How to Tie Freshwater Flies

How to Tie Freshwater Flies

KENNETH E. BAY

Photographs by Matthew M. Vinciguerra

WINCHESTER PRESS

Library of Congress Catalog Card Number: 74-78706
ISBN: 0-87691-148-3

Published by Winchester Press
460 Park Avenue, New York 10022

Printed in the United States of America

To my wife, Jeanne, who patiently sat by for
many long weekends while this book was in
preparation and supplied vital inspiration and
labor when I most needed it.

Contents

Introduction

THIS IS A BOOK WHICH CAN BE USED BY THE WOULD-BE FLY-TIER to learn how to tie flies without personal instruction. Even if you are a fly-tier with some experience, you too will find that there are numerous tips in the instructions that will shed light on many operations that can be troublesome.

I have instructed fly-tying students for many years (more than I wish to recall) and have avidly read all published works on this subject, hoping to enhance my teaching ability. I have become increasingly aware that to date, no attempt has been made to do a basic fly-tying book that shows how to tie representative trout flies in clear larger-than-life photographic sequences. Such a book is needed. And so here I have presented a system of fly-tying, showing clearly all of the steps necessary to tie all of the basic flies we use in our fishing.

The book is based on long observation of my own students, and it also reflects the opinion of sages of fly-tying whom I had the privilege of being associated with during my early years at the vise. Among these gentlemen were such as Irv Lacey, Herb Howard, and Chuck Conrad (all of whom now fish in different waters). Their names reflect happily in the memories of great numbers of today's fly-fishermen, from coast to coast.

If you can tie a shoelace, you can tie a fly. Fly-tying looks harder than it is. Unless you have four thumbs, there's no reason why you can't learn to tie flies that will catch fish as successfully as any you can buy; and you can learn in a very short time, once you have set your mind to it.

Leaving aside bass bugs, there are four basic types of artificial flies, none of them requiring any special skill or dexterity

1

to tie. They are: bucktails and streamers; wet flies; dry flies; and nymphs.

The nymph is often included among wet flies, though it has more generally been considered a distinct type in recent years. For that matter, any fly fished under the surface can be considered a wet fly. That includes bucktails and streamers, but because they are meant to imitate small baitfish rather than aquatic insects, they have traditionally been given a classification of their own.

This book has a chapter on each of the above categories. The flies selected, fourteen of them in total, were the result of quite some study and consultation. My intention was to select flies that would illustrate 95 to 98 percent of all the procedures the fly-tier would ever need. Other lesser-used procedures, if you find them desirable for your flies, you will either learn through your own ingenuity or by observation of different fly types. But if you have assimilated the contents of these chapters, you will be ready for more esoteric techniques and could well originate new procedures on your own—as happens often with fly-tiers. That is one of the pleasures of the activity.

In this course of instruction, you must first and foremost master the three basic procedures which are detailed in Chapter 4. If you don't, you will be handicapped when you try to follow the steps of tying the actual flies.

When I was in the Air Force many years ago, our gunnery instructor stated that we had to learn to "field-strip" (disassemble and reassemble) a 50-caliber machine gun while blindfolded. This seemed preposterous at the time. However, after diligent application, I and others in the class accomplished this with great pride—and the ability served us well in times to come.

You will find that fly-tying consists primarily of basic procedures, and if you do not learn them cold, the craft will always be a chore—not the relaxing pleasure that it should be. So—*learn the basic procedures* before progressing to Chapters 5 through 8.

Many of you fly-fishermen will recognize that the flies tied in the photographic sequences are not necessarily on the size of hooks you prefer. In the interest of photographic clarity of detail, the hook sizes are of the largest practical sizes for the flies shown, to a size 10, which is not too often fished here in Eastern streams. However, the pattern descriptions of each fly preceding the chapters will indicate the general range of hook sizes in which each fly is regularly tied and fished.

Every book treating the art of fly-tying makes a genuine effort to enable the tier to visualize the basic materials commonly used and the finished flies. Thanks to Matty Vinciguerra's photographic talent, we have included color plates, fourteen portraying the flies discussed in the book and five depicting various types of quills, feathers, and furs. Completely accurate color reproduction is virtually impossible with fly-tying materials, but the plates are at least good approximations of the real items.

Although I was fortunate to learn my fly-tying by personal instruction, there have been many times when I felt it necessary to refer to written works of others. I wish to share with you my taste in books, and so have listed a few in the Appendix. They will be most helpful, not only in fly-tying but also to give you a little exposure in entomology—a necessary adjunct to tying flies. My list by no means covers the field, but it consists of books which have my respect. The list will be a good starting point for you. The Appendix also includes a list of suppliers of tools and materials for fly-tying.

So now you can get started in a venerable and enjoyable art that will never leave you. You might even tie your first fly tonight and catch a trout on it tomorrow. Do not be surprised.

I would like to communicate one other thought as you begin your fly-tying career: There are flies that are tied so that other fishermen can admire their perfection, and there are flies that are tied for your own fishing. I prefer the latter. So do not lose your perspective.

Best of luck.

Kenneth E. Bay
May 1974

1
Work Area
and Tools

THE MOST IMPORTANT TOOLS YOU WILL USE IN FLY-TYING
are your hands, for it is essentially a manual operation. Beyond
your hands, you will need only a few items of equipment and
tools, some of which you may find around the house. Here's
a checklist of what you will need:

1. Work table
2. Work lamp
3. Tying vise
4. Scissors
5. Hackle pliers
6. Bobbin
7. Bodkin or dubbing needle

If you're going to be tying fairly frequently, it's best to set up
a work area where you can keep tools and materials in one place.
With this kind of a set-up, sitting down and tying is no bother,
whether it's for a half-hour before dinner or a three-hour session
on a Saturday afternoon. Besides, tiers sometimes get messy and
it's a lot easier to tidy up if you limit your work area.

However, this kind of a work arrangement isn't always possible, particularly in a city apartment. Don't let that discourage
you. It simply means organizing a little differently. Find a place
to store your materials and tools when not in use—a closet shelf
is a good place. Materials such as feathers and furs should be
kept in mothproof containers anyway, so it's no big project to
bring them out when you're in the mood to tie.

Let's take the seven items of equipment one at a time.

Work table The first piece of equipment you'll need is a work
table, often called a tying bench, even if it's only a kitchen table.

Professional tiers turning out flies in volume often do work at benches, and the term has been adopted generally.

There really are no hard-and-fast rules on what a work table needs to be, except that it should be one that you can sit comfortably at and that provides the work space you need. It ought to be at least 24×36 inches, and 36×54 inches is better. But if other factors, such as limited room space, have to be considered, then use whatever size fits. Professional tiers can work at a table no more than 24 inches square with no trouble. They can do it because everything is highly organized, with materials preselected and prepared so they can work swiftly and smoothly with no lost time or motion.

Whatever else it is, your table must be sturdy and firm. A rickety table is an abomination in tying flies; nothing will drive you up the wall as surely as having the table wobble or vibrate when you're in the middle of a crucial tying operation. Be sure the table is steady.

The table surface should be smooth and of a light shade. Most of the materials you will work with, including hooks, are difficult to see against a dark background. If your tabletop is dark you can paint it a light color, being sure to use a flat paint, not glossy. Or you can cover the tabletop with vinyl sheeting or adhesive shelf paper.

Whatever you use to cover the surface, make sure it has a dull finish that won't reflect light. Working over a shiny surface is hard on the eyes and extremely fatiguing.

Lacking a table you can call your own, your best bet is a piece of plywood cut to the size you need, which can be stored away when not in use. The board should be at least a half-inch thick.

Other possibilities are a desk, or the dining-room table if you can get away with it.

Work lamp The greatest boon for fly-tiers since the discovery of electricity is the high-intensity lamp. No experienced tier would think of working without proper lighting; beginners often do. I have seen them hunched over a vise, straining their eyes under light from a ceiling fixture six or eight feet away.

Until recently, the standby of fly-tiers was the old-fashioned gooseneck lamp, and it wasn't bad. Many thousand flies have been tied under its glare, and if you happen to have one around the house, you could do worse. But if you want to do better, get yourself a high-intensity lamp. They are available in a variety of shapes, sizes, and prices, and many are ideal for fly-tying. Prices run from under $10 to $40 or more, but since this is an essential piece of equipment, get the best you can afford. It will last a long time and you'll bless it every time you sit down to tie.

The unique feature of the high-intensity lamp is that it focuses a narrow cone of highly concentrated light wherever you aim it. With a proper size bulb — at least the equivalent of 100 watts — eyestrain is eliminated and you can see exactly what you're doing as you tie.

Place the lamp behind the vise and to the right, with the shade at a fairly high angle and at least six or eight inches from the vise so you don't knock into it with your hand as you work. Eventually, your personal comfort and needs will dictate the best position for the lamp.

Tying vise People were tying flies long before the vise was available. The method was — and still is — known as tying in the hand. The tier holds the hook in one hand and uses his teeth, knees, and any other part of his body that will help. The method is still in use by many professional tiers in Scotland and even a few in this country.

The easy way to do it, however, is with a vise. A vise is simply a tool for gripping and holding an object in its jaws, in this case a fly hook. Vises available offer fairly similar clamping principles, with the jaws of varying profiles, operated by a cam-lever or rotating knob at the rear of the collet or shaft. Prices run from about $10 to about $20, with some specialized models going up to $25. One of the most popular vises sells for under $15. It will pay you to look through the catalogs.

The most popular models are also adjustable for height. Some models offer additional features, which many tiers find desirable. These include a feature that allows the vise to rotate completely, angle adjustment, and a right- or left-hand adjustment.

A vise usually is equipped with a clamp for attaching it to the table, making it easy to remove for storage. A few, mostly portable models, can be secured to a board, and if you're interested in a tying set-up that will travel, you might take a look at those.

A useful accessory for your vise is a material clip. The clip fastens to the vise and can be positioned to hold materials out of the way while you are working on some other part of the fly.

Look for a vise that is well made, with the jaws machined from hardened steel. All moving parts, such as the cam-lever, also should be made of hardened steel to resist wear and mushrooming. The jaws should grip a hook firmly, allowing no movement while under tension from the tying thread.

Chances are you'll only buy one vise in a lifetime, and if it meets the requirements above, you won't need more than one.

Scissors   The matter of scissors can be summed up in three words: Get two pairs. You may use one a lot more than the other, but you need both.

One pair will do all of the fine work, such as snipping thread, trimming body or wing materials close to the hook, and

any other delicate cutting called for. For this kind of work, the scissors should be small, with pointed blades and very sharp. These come with either straight or curved blades, and which you choose is up to you.

Your second pair should be larger and sturdier. That's the pair for cutting bucktail, tinsel, heavy-quilled feathers, lead wire for weighting flies, and anything else too heavy for the smaller scissors.

You can't do fine cutting with dull scissors, so keep those blades sharp at all times, if you want to turn out neat, tight flies. You can have the blades sharpened regularly by a professional cutlery sharpener (your barber can help you locate one if the Yellow Pages can't). Or you can do it yourself, using a good oil-stone.

Hackle pliers   Years ago, before there were store-bought hackle pliers available, tiers made do with wooden spring-style clothes-pins. They weren't very satisfactory, but there was little choice. Nowadays, you have quite a choice.

Hackle pliers are essentially spring-loaded forceps which open by finger pressure. Chief differences are in size, weight of metal, and length of nose or jaws—the part that grips the feather. They run somewhere between $1 and $4 in price.

You'll find your pliers come in handy for any number of little jobs, but their main function is in winding hackles. We'll

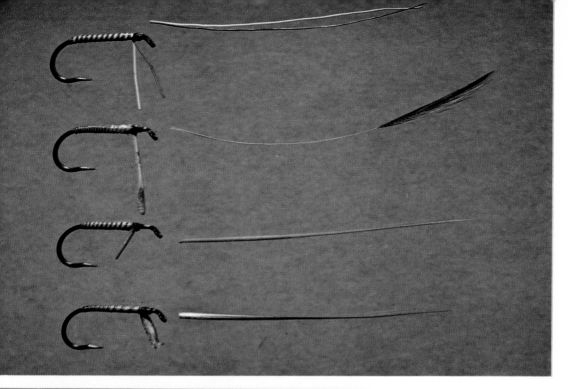

QUILLS

Top to bottom:
Black-and-white moose mane
Brown hackle stem, stripped
Peacock quill, stripped
Yellow dyed condor quill, stripped

HACKLE FEATHERS

Left column, from top:
cree; badger; dyed blue
dun; multi-variant; red-
brown; ginger variant;
cochy-bondhu. *Center:*
spade hackle, brown;
badger variant, saddle
hackle. *Right:* natural dark-
blue dun; cream; dark
ginger; grizzly; light ginger;
Coachman brown; dyed
rusty dun.

DUBBING FURS

Left column, top to bottom: common rabbit; muskrat; cream fitch. *Center:* hare's ear with half of mask. *Right:* red fox underbelly; beaver; otter.

QUILL FEATHERS

Top row, left to right: yellow dyed mallard primary; hen pheasant; male pheasant tail; natural mallard primary. *Bottom:* dark turkey; cinnamon turkey.

BODY FEATHERS

Top row, left to right: widgeon; brown partridge; golden pheasant; yellow dyed mallard. *Center:* mallard flank; bronze mallard. *Bottom:* gray partridge; guinea fowl; teal; wood-duck flank.

THE FLIES

Here are color photographs of all the flies in this book, in the same order in which they are presented in the text. As I have warned already in the Introduction, it is very difficult to capture the true colors of fly-tying materials on film, and this problem is compounded in filming actual flies that combine several materials, some shiny, some iridescent, some flat. So you may find that your flies, tied according to instructions with the proper materials, vary slightly from these.

Black Nose Dace bucktail

Black Ghost streamer

Dark Cahill wet fly

Leadwing Coachman wet fly

Brown Bivisible dry fly

Quill Gordon dry fly

Female Beaverkill dry fly

Irresistible dry fly

Adams Spentwing dry fly

Caddis Fly dry fly

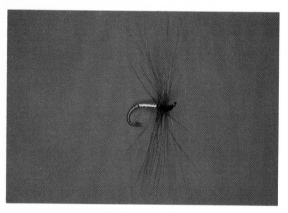

Spider dry fly

Floss Body nymph

Hare's Ear nymph

Quill Body Emerger nymph

get into hackles a little further along, but they are basically the feathers you use to imitate legs on dry flies, beards or whiskers on wets, and tails. Particularly for winding dry-fly hackle, a long nose is an advantage. It's a good idea, though not essential, to work with two pairs — a small one for your tiny flies and a larger one for the bigger flies. However, if you get one of the long-nosed models, even in medium size, it will handle any hackle feather you work with.

The gripping surfaces of your pliers should be scored or serrated so feathers won't slip out while you're winding. Make sure the jaws don't have sharp edges that will cut through the feathers.

Bobbin If you've ever spent any time around sewing machines you'll know that a bobbin is simply a thread holder. You don't actually need a bobbin to tie flies; it's possible to tie without one. Not all tiers use a bobbin, but it does make it easier for the beginner to handle the thread and it keeps constant tension on the thread throughout the tying operation.

One of the keys to a well-made fly is tight, even thread winding, and to do that the thread has to be kept under tension every step of the way. Without a bobbin it's difficult for the beginner to maintain that tension and concentrate on three or four other operations at the same time. When you let go of the thread, the weight of the bobbin hanging loose is enough to keep it from unwinding or loosening.

All bobbins are designed for the same job, so they're all styled more or less the same. Some are plastic, others metal, and they all cost about the same. Whatever model you decide on, it should be capable of holding any standard-size spool of tying thread. Some adjust to various sizes, a feature you may desire.

The thread is fed from the spool through a thin tube, out the top and to the hook. One of the great challenges in tying is preventing the thread from slipping back through that tiny tunnel. Trying to feed the thread up through the tube is one of the most frustrating chores ever conceived. Inserting a loop of fine wire from the top of the bobbin tube to catch the thread and pull it through solves this problem. The wax from the tying thread eventually builds up inside the tube, and it's a good idea to clean it out every once in a while. You can do this with a straightened paperclip.

Bodkin (dubbing needle) It may be that the last time you encountered the word "bodkin" was when you were reading fairy tales. If your memory is sharp you'll recall that a bodkin was nothing but a needle on which a princess pricked her finger, inducing her to sink into a long-term slumber. Well, a bodkin is still nothing but a needle with a handle, but it's a mighty handy gadget for tying flies. It also travels under the name "dubbing needle."

You can buy a bodkin or take a couple of minutes and make one. To make one, take a long hatpin or needle—at least three inches long—and simply push the blunt end into a cork or wood handle, and you're in business. It will be more comfortable and easier to work with if the whole thing is four to six inches long.

If you want to get fancy you can buy a bodkin with a metal or plastic handle. Some have the point magnetized, which is useful for picking up hooks.

Often while you're working on a fly, feather or fur fibers or other materials get caught under the tying thread and are bound down. When this happens, you use the bodkin point to pick out the bound fibers.

The bodkin point is also handy for picking out fibers from a fur body when you want a rough-finished body, such as some nymphs call for.

And, not least, the bodkin point is the best implement around for placing tiny drops of head cement to finish off your fly. It's better than the smallest brush.

Head cement, thread, and wax The next chapter discusses fly-tying materials in some detail, but it is appropriate to mention a few of them here along with other basic equipment.

Having your fly unravel or the wings shift in the middle of a "hatch" when fish are on a feeding spree is guaranteed to leave you frustrated, to say the least. Believe me, it happens, and it usually happens because the fly wasn't constructed properly. A couple of simple precautions at the tying bench will help prevent that kind of disaster.

The first thing is to make sure all materials are anchored firmly to the hook. That means tying everything down firmly at every step. I find it also helps if you spread a very little cement along the bare hook before you start tying in materials. Begin tying while the cement is still wet, but be sure there's very little cement on the hook, otherwise the materials will become soaked with it and the fly will be ruined even before you've finished it. Do it right, though, and you'll end up with flies that will hold together no matter how hard you fish them.

When a fly begins to come apart, it's usually at the head, and it happens for one of two reasons, sometimes both. One is that the wrapping isn't snug enough; the other is that the head wasn't cemented properly. Keep the head small and wrap it as tightly as you can. Then apply your cement. You only need a tiny drop, but make certain it covers the head completely. If there's any doubt in your mind, let it dry and then give it a second coat. I'm still fishing with flies tied years ago following this procedure, and they're as sound as the day they came off the vise.

Silk thread has been the standard binding in fly-tying for at least five hundred years, and it's still No. 1 with many tiers. However, modern technology has created synthetics that are ideal for fly-tying, offering the advantages of silk, plus additional qualities of their own.

For one thing, the synthetics incorporate extremely fine diameters and great strength. And since the thread is not twisted, it lies flat, helping to eliminate the bulky build-up caused by repeated windings.

Tying thread should be waxed to help hold it in place when wrapped around hook shank or materials. For years waxing was strictly a do-it-yourself chore, and what a chore it was! It didn't leave much time for tying. Fortunately, all that is in the past, because spools of pre-waxed thread, both silk and synthetics, are now readily available.

But there are times when you'll need more wax on your thread than it comes with, and that's when your fly calls for a dubbed fur body. For this, tiny bits of fur or fur fibers are rolled onto a piece of thread to form a "rope" of fur. This rope is then wound around the hook shank to form the body. It's a simple enough operation if the fur sticks to the thread. What makes it stick is wax—sticky wax. You can buy wax in small cans, which is the easy way to do it. To work properly, the wax has to be soft and sticky.

More than likely, between your tying sessions, your wax will lose its surface stickiness when it gets cold. If so, it may be warmed by placing it near your lamp for a short while, or possibly just your hand warmth for a few minutes will be enough to restore it, after which it can be kneaded between thumb and forefinger.

Buying tools and materials   The best way to buy your materials and tools is to walk into a store and pick out what you want. Not all tiers are handy to such suppliers, however, and they have to rely on mail-order supply houses. Fortunately, there are a sizable number of such firms around the country, and in the main the quality of the materials they offer is high. If you stick with the better brand names in tools and equipment, it really doesn't matter where you buy them, except for small differences in prices. Many of the mail-order houses publish catalogs, and it will pay you to send for them. Many are well illustrated and, among other things, it's a good way to become familiar with tools and materials. A list, by no means complete, of mail-order supply firms will be found at the back of this book. Others will be found in fly-fishing and outdoor magazines.

2
Hooks and Materials

WE KNOW THAT A TROUT FLY WAS TIED AND FISHED IN MACE-
donia nearly two thousand years ago, and it was tied on a hook,
basically very much like the hooks you use, though cruder. The
last two thousand years have brought refinements to fishhooks,
but little change in the basic design. Interestingly, most fly hooks
are imported from England and Norway, though plenty of
general-purpose hooks are made in the U.S.A.

Like most items for fishing, hooks are made in a number of
styles and varieties, each best suited for a particular job. In fly-
tying, you'll be concerned primarily with these three styles:

Model Perfect Bend. This has a uniformly round bend—the
curved part of the hook—and it's the most popular hook for
dry flies, though sometimes it's used for wet flies and
nymphs too.

Sproat Bend. This has a parabolic bend and is used mostly
for wet flies, as it is generally of heavier wire, which helps
weight the fly.

Limerick Bend. This has an even more pronounced parabolic bend than the Sproat Bend. It is usually found in long-
shanked hooks used for streamers and bucktails.

Fly hooks are made either with a down-turned eye or an upturned eye. Most of the flies you will tie call for a down-turned
eye, in which the eye is angled downward from the hook shank.
Upturned-eye hooks are generally used for very small dry
flies—size 20 and smaller. In those smaller sizes, the upturned
eye provides better hooking.

There are good reasons—and hundreds of years of develop-
ment behind those reasons—why today's fly hooks are designed

as they are. Take the Limerick, the hook recommended for streamers and bucktails, which are meant to imitate small baitfish. Small baitfish are long and thin; Limerick hooks are long and they come in various lengths. The length of the hook is designated by a number and the letter X; 6X or 8X, for example. What this means is that the hook is six or eight additional sizes longer than the standard hook length.

In tying wet flies or nymphs, you're imitating or trying to create the impression of an aquatic insect at an underwater stage of its life, or of a drowning insect. For this you need a hook made of heavy wire, or you may tie thin lead wire on the hook shank before building the body, so it will sink readily and stay beneath the surface in a heavy current.

Dry flies are tied to represent the adult stage of aquatic insects or certain terrestrials—land-based insects that are blown or fall into the water—that float on the surface. In the adult stage, aquatic insects float along the top of the water before they fly off, and fish rise to feed on them. Obviously, your fly has to float if it is to imitate these insects, which means the hook it's tied on must be made of the lightest steel consistent with strength, and hook manufacturers have delivered in grand style on this requirement. Some dry-fly hooks described as 3X fine wire are so light you can almost blow one off your hand.

The next time you pick up a fly hook, think about how far it has come in the last two thousand years, and you'll view it with new respect.

MATERIALS

The unknown Macedonian who tied the first-known trout fly a couple of thousand years ago simply wrapped some wool around the shank, lashed a couple of yellow—wax-colored, he called it—feathers to the hook, and threw it out. It caught trout, but maybe they were easier to fool in those days. In any case, fishermen since that time have never let up in their search for materials to use in tying flies. Probably no fowl, animal, or plant has escaped the endless seeking for materials to create the perfect fly. Today's fly-tier is confronted with a vast, bewildering array of feathers, furs, tinsels, hairs, fibers, and who knows what else when he sits down to sort out the ingredients for an artificial that will dupe a fish into thinking it's something tasty and nourishing. It can be confusing, but it needn't be.

Essentially, you'll be working with feathers and furs, with things like tinsel, thread, floss, and other materials in a minor role. You'll run into words like quill, hackle, herl. Stripped of their regal titles they stand exposed as nothing more than feathers. Fancy feathers, perhaps, but feathers nonetheless.

If you're a hunter, chances are you're already familiar with many feathers and furs. Otherwise, you may not know a wood-duck flank feather from peacock herl, both of which you'll run into many times in fly-tying. There really is no shortcut to learning to identify the different feathers and furs that go into flies. The best way to learn to recognize them is to look at them and work with them.

There is one way to speed up this educational process, though, and that is buying a fly-tying kit, which a number of supply houses are now offering. The better kits include all the essentials to get started in this branch of fly-fishing—materials and tools. What is important to you at this stage is that the materials are labeled, which means you can pick up a peacock sword, for example, which is clearly identified, and from then on you know what a peacock sword looks like. No kit contains the full range of materials you may work with as you go along, but most contain the basics, and that's enough to get you started.

Prices vary on these kits according to what they contain and the quality of the materials and tools included. It's been my experience that the materials and tools offered in most kits are of good quality, and you can save money. I did a cost breakdown on one kit that was priced at $44. The items included, if bought individually, would cost about $65. A typical kit will contain a good vise and other essential tools, such as hackle pliers, scissors, bobbin, plus an adequate supply of feathers, furs, yarns, tinsel, tying thread, cement, etc., all clearly labeled for easy identification.

In addition to the kits, you can learn a lot about materials, as you can about tools and equipment for that matter, by studying catalogs, many of which are well illustrated. Other books on fly-tying and materials are helpful, too.

Tying materials are usually classified according to the part of a fly where they will be used. The number of main sections of an artificial fly will vary, depending on the type. The major components are body, wings, tails, and legs. Listed below are some of the materials most commonly used:

Body materials

Wool yarns
Synthetic yarns
Silk floss
Synthetic flosses
Animal hairs
Animal furs
Tinsel—fine, medium, and wide widths
Quills from large feathers
Quills from peacock tail feathers
Raffia
Chenille
Porcupine quills
Moose mane

Wing and tail materials

Duck quill feathers
Bucktail and deer hair
Wood-duck flank feathers or imitations
Mallard flank feathers
Synthetic yarns
Marabou feathers
Calf tail (impala)
Partridge feathers
Peacock herl
Animal hairs
Feather fibers

Leg materials

Animal hairs
Feather fibers

This list doesn't begin to come close to the literally hundreds of different substances used in flies, and new materials are being discovered or concocted every day. It does cover materials for the basic patterns we'll be dealing with in this book, however. As you become more proficient in your tying, your own imagination and ingenuity will lead you to other materials and ways to use those listed above. It can also serve as a guide in buying materials for getting started.

Quills What I remember most clearly about my early tying days is my bewilderment at trying to make some sense out of tying and material terms. Most confusing to me were the quills. A glance at the list above will show three separate references to quills for bodies and another for wings. Since you'll be running into quills frequently in your tying, it might be worthwhile to take a minute to explain them.

The best way to go about this is to pick up a feather — say, a feather from the wing of a duck, swan, turkey, or other fowl. You'll notice that a hollow tube runs the length of the feather; you're probably holding the feather at the end of this tube or stem. That's a quill.

If it is a broad feather, segments can be cut from it, for use as wings for a wet or dry fly (as well as nymph wing cases). It is then also known as a wing quill. If this feather was taken from a mallard duck, you would find it listed in your fly-tying catalog as a duck or mallard quill.

Another variety of quill is that which is obtained from the stem of a small feather, such as a hackle feather. This feather can be stripped of all its fibers to leave a bare stem and used to wrap on the hook for a body which appears to have segmentations, as do most aquatic insects.

Birds contribute still other quills, which are made from a single wide fiber removed from the stem of large feathers of such birds as the condor, turkey, and peacock. This fiber can be stripped of the fuzz along its length and used to create another segmented-appearing body. Many tiers also use these quills with the fuzz left on to create impressionistic flies.

Animals are a source of an entirely different-appearing quill, as can be seen in the case of porcupines and peccary. These are hollow spines useful in the form taken from the hide for fly bodies, tails, and sometimes legs in nymphs.

Hackles Not quite as confusing as quills, but still presenting some difficulties, are hackles. A hackle is a feather. In its strictest definition, a hackle is a long, slender feather from the neck of a rooster or a hen. In fly-tying, the definition has been stretched to include feathers from the back of a rooster, known as saddle hackles. Actually, today the term "hackle" refers not so much to the origin of a feather as to how it is used on the fly; if it is used as hackle, it's called a hackle feather.

Hackles are used in every type of fly. They're used as wings in streamers, as legs in both wet and dry flies, as beards on wets, and as tails in all types. In dry flies tied without wings, the hackle serves as both legs and wings. If you begin to get the idea that hackles rank pretty high in fly-tying, you're right on target. It's the one subject that gets more batting around among fly-fishermen and tiers than probably anything else in the game.

General Ulysses S. Grant once allowed that he knew two tunes: One was "Yankee Doodle" and the other wasn't. As far as fly-tiers are concerned, with respect to hackle quality it's pretty much the same: There's a dry-fly grade, and there's everything else. But fly-tiers can, at least, make a case for their prejudice.

A dry fly has to float high and dry along the top of the water, with no part of it except the legs—that is, the hackle—and in most cases the tail touching the surface. This means the hackle must have the strength and stiffness to support the weight of the fly and keep it perched up there on its toes. Only top-grade, high-quality cock hackle will do that. And it gets scarcer and harder to come by every year, to say nothing of what's happening to prices. But prime-grade hackle is available, if you take the trouble to search it out.

With wet flies, you want to go the other way: Look for soft hackle. Hen hackle is best, though poor-grade cock hackle works well, too. On wet flies, you want hackle for legs or beards that will wave and undulate in the current as the fly moves underwater, because that's the way it is with the natural insects. Fortunately, there's plenty of this kind of hackle around and prices are way below the cost of first-quality dry-fly hackle.

Wet or dry, the best way to buy hackle is by the neck, either whole or by the piece. For dries, the whole neck is best, as your chances of getting the tiny feathers for small flies are better, as well as a wider range of sizes. A neck is just what the name implies: the skin of the back of the neck of a rooster or hen with feathers attached. The smallest feathers are found close to the top of the head of the bird. The ability to judge accurately the quality of a neck is something that comes with experience. Until you've acquired it, it's a good idea to have an experienced friend do the picking-out for you. Otherwise, you'll have to rely on the knowledge and honesty of a dealer.

In any case, there are a couple of things to look for in selecting hackle. First, look for a gloss or sheen on the feathers. On high-grade hackle this glossiness is quite pronounced and obvious. Don't waste your time or money on dull, listless-looking feathers for dry flies; such feathers are useful for wets, but you shouldn't pay high-quality hackle prices for them. Next, check the feathers for springiness and life. Take a feather and bend it sideways, then let go of the tip. It should spring back into shape instantly and the fibers or barbs should mesh back into their original position, leaving no gaps in the feather. And, finally, make sure the neck contains feathers in the sizes you'll need for the fly sizes you'll be tying. Large hackles are never a problem; you'll find plenty on any neck. It's the midge hackles that are harder to come by, and if you're figuring on tying flies in size 18 and smaller, examine the neck closely. Often a neck will contain small feathers—that is, *short* feathers—that nevertheless have fibers that are quite long, and a hackle which looks as though it ought to be size 18 or 20 or smaller actually measures out to size 14 or 16. In other words, length of the feather is not what determines its fly size; length of the fiber does.

Saddle hackles, found at the back end of cocks, are often overlooked for dry flies, but shouldn't be. Some very fine hackle is to be found in saddles, and it's ideal for larger-sized dry flies and spiders. Saddles are also first choice for streamer wings because of their length.

One other thing to look for is the amount of web on a hackle. Web is the fuzz found on the base of hackle fibers emanating outward from the stem. Web is OK on wet flies because it is water-absorbent. Obviously, this trait is a disadvantage for dry flies. So, in dry flies, the less web, the better. The highest grade of hackle has the least web.

A whole book could easily be written on the subject of hackle colors—in fact, a number have. Books like that remind me of the little girl who expressed some curiosity about penguins and received a five-inch-thick encyclopedia about them from her grandmother. In her thank-you note she wrote that she appreciated the gift, but it was more than she really wanted to know about penguins. Nonetheless, it's helpful to have some basic knowledge about hackle colors. One thing you'll discover when you begin buying hackle is that there is a definite relation between color and price. And, of course, the colors in greatest demand are the highest-priced.

There are dozens of colors and shades or variations of colors in hackle, but for our purposes we won't need to go into more than a few of the most commonly used.

White. Pure white in quality necks is hard to come by. Even in its highest grade, white hackle is usually dull, chalky, and soft-textured, with limited use in dry flies. Most of the so-called white necks you'll come across are actually off-white or shades of cream. Their biggest use is for dyeing into other colors.

Ginger. Hackle in a range of tannish buff. Is much used in tying.

Brown. A color covering a wide range of shades and hues as used by tiers. In red-mahogany, it is known as Coachman brown, a greatly desired shade, but rare in top grade because of its soft texture. Most brown hackle you'll see is the general color of a Rhode Island Red fowl, often referred to as red or red-brown. This is one of the most-used colors in tying.

Dun. The aristocrat of hackle, prime-quality dun hackle is the most sought-after and difficult to find. Actually, dun is not a specific color but rather a range of shades of blue-gray-bronze. In fly-tying the definition of dun has been extended to include honey dun, olive dun, rusty dun, and several other shades in addition to blue dun, the shade by which it is best known. The only thing certain about dun hackle is that no two necks will be exactly the same shade. You'll have to pick out the precise tint you want.

Grizzly. Sometimes called barred rock because it comes from the Plymouth Rock cock. In its most desirable form the feather has alternate, even bars of black and white. A highly useful hackle that is becoming scarcer, largely because of the universal shift to white leghorns for eggs and table birds. A prime grizzly neck now sells for as much as top-grade blue dun, and sometimes more.

Badger. A feather with a black center stripe running full length, found in a range of colors from white to cream.

Furnace. Has the same black center stripe as badger, but comes in shades of brown rather than cream.

The scarcity of high-grade natural blue dun and grizzly hackle mentioned above naturally raises the question of what to do about it, since so many of the popular patterns call for one or the other. In the case of grizzly, there's not much you can do except pay the price to obtain quality. In the case of the dun colors, however, the picture is much brighter. The solution is dyed hackle. The art of hackle-dyeing has come a long way and dyed hackle can be an excellent substitute for the natural, provided, of course, the dyeing is first-class and the feathers are top-grade. I frequently use dyed hackle and, by and large, find it completely satisfactory.

Herl A herl is a single strand of fuzzy appearance, taken from the tail feathers of such birds as peacock, ostrich, and emu. Peacock herl is used both in its natural fuzzy state and also stripped of the fuzz for other purposes, primarily quill bodies. Ostrich and emu herl is usually used without removing the fuzzy fibers. Fuzzy herl is used to create the appearance of bulk, as in tying the Leadwing Coachman (Chapter 6).

When desired for a quill body, a strand of herl is selected from the eye at the top of the tail feather, and the fuzz is removed to leave a flat ribbonlike quill, which can then be wrapped on the fly body. This procedure is described in detail in the instructions for tying the Quill Gordon dry fly (Chapter 7). It is again utilized for the Quill Body Emerger nymph (Chapter 8).

3
Getting Started

IF YOU WERE TO SIT HALF A DOZEN EXPERT FLY-TIERS AT A TABLE and tell them all to tie a fly of the same pattern — let's say a Dark Cahill — it's a safe bet each one would go about it in slightly different fashion. Yet, when finished, all six flies would be well-made, exact representations of a Dark Cahill.

All of which proves — what? That there are more ways to skin a cat than by cramming Grade A cream into its gullet. And while few flies call for cat fur these days, cat's whiskers were often used by tiers a few centuries ago.

Which brings me to the point of this chapter. Fly-tying in this country had its origin in the East, more specifically in the Catskills of New York State, where such giants as Reuben Cross and Theodore Gordon plied their trade, and gave birth to what has become known as the Catskill School of tying. Out of that school have come others, and today there are as many schools of tying as there are regions of the country.

Now, I'm not about to advocate any one school of tying. But because I learned to tie in the New York area, I was most influenced by the so-called Herb Howard School, also known as the Ray Bergman School, since Bergman and Howard worked together for many years. So the procedures and techniques I will deal with in this book are what might be called the Herb Howard style of tying, not because I think it's better, but simply because it's my style. Then, too, it will help maintain a uniformity of style which will make it easier for the beginning tier. Eventually, as you gain experience and confidence in your own ability, you will develop your own personal techniques and tying tricks.

Anyway, differences among tiers are minor — a matter of how one tier wraps a body or winds a hackle in Maryland as against the method used by a tier in the Northwest. The point is, both will turn out well-made, excellent, and effective flies. And that's what counts, after all. The thing to remember is not to get so involved in styles and techniques that you forget fly-tying is supposed to be fun as much as anything else. Your purpose in tying is to produce flies that will be fun to fish and that will catch fish for you.

My first thought was to title this chapter "Fly-Tying Orientation," but that sounded too much like the first day at boot camp, so I decided to call it simply what it is: "Getting Started." And a good way to go about it, I think, is to cover some procedures and terms that apply to fly-tying in general. That way, we can eliminate the need to repeat them in each chapter.

It's important that correct proportions be observed in your tying, particularly with dry flies, where proportions are standard. The rules are simple:

Tail. The tail length should be equal to the distance from behind the eye of the hook to the beginning of the bend.

Hackle. Same length as the tail.

Wings. The wings should extend above the hackle in the finished fly. Therefore, wing length should be equal to the distance from the eye of the hook to the rearmost extension of the bend.

Since there are variations in proportions for streamers, bucktails, and wet flies, they will be covered in tying instructions for those types. Some procedures are pretty much standard, and it's helpful if you learn them at the outset. It will make it easier to follow the steps illustrated in the following chapters.

Materials such as floss, tinsel, dubbed bodies, hackles, etc., should be tied in *beneath* the hook shank. Hold material at a 60–75° angle while tying in.

Always wrap over and away from you. In a head-on view this would be clockwise for a right-handed tier, counter-clockwise for a left-hander.

Wings and tails are always tied on the top side of the hook shank.

Two phrases which will be repeated in the instructions are "tie in" and "tie off." "Tying in" is the fastening of any material to the hook with the tying thread. "Tying off" refers to cutting off the excess of any material after it has been secured on the hook with the tying thread.

The surest way to a tight, neat head is to use a whip finish. It takes a little practice to get the hang of the whip finish, but once you learn, it's as fast as any other method and does a better job.

4
Basic Fly-tying Procedures

I HAVE DIVIDED THE MOST BASIC FLY-TYING PROCEDURES INTO three categories: making the jam knot and putting on the tail; tying on the wing materials, for both wet and dry flies; and making the whip finish. Each operation is explained in the photograph sequences that follow in this chapter, and once you master them you will be ready to begin tying actual flies.

Remember that a very light coating of head cement on the bare hook before you begin tying will help ensure a well-made fly. However, if you run through each of these procedures several times to make sure you have the hang of them, omit the cement so that you won't make a mess and can reuse the same thread and hook.

PROCEDURE 1: MAKING THE JAM KNOT AND PUTTING ON THE TAIL

1 The jam knot is simply the act of making one turn of thread with the right hand, over itself, to hold it tight. To start, hold the thread in position with the left hand and the bobbin as shown here. Hold it firmly so that when the strand is passed over with the right hand it will hold the thread in position.

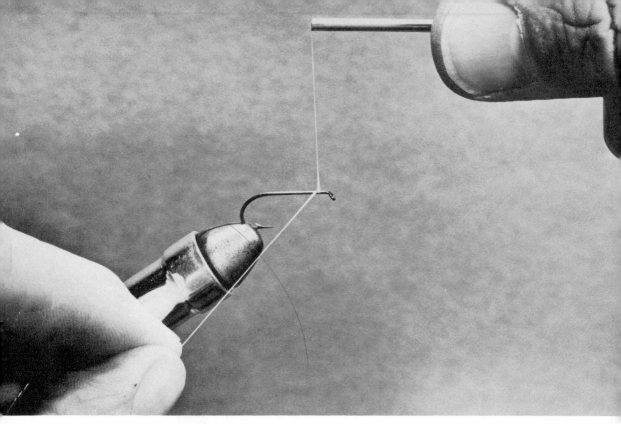

2 Here the right hand, holding the bobbin, traps the thread in position on the hook shank.

3 A number of turns are completed down the shank, positively securing the thread. Next, snip off the strand formerly held with the left hand.

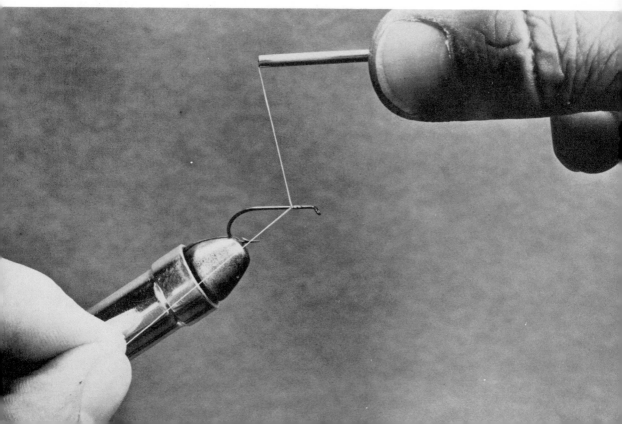

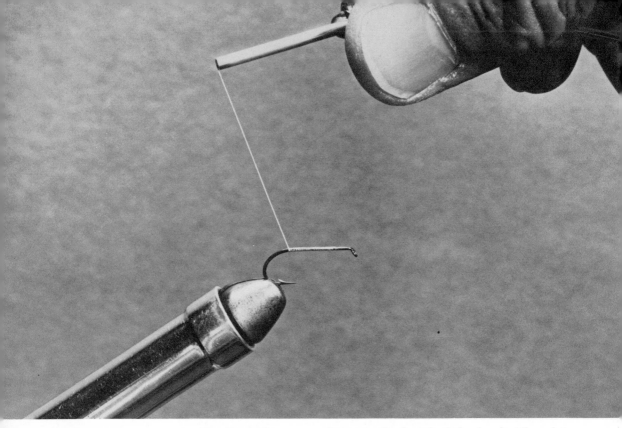

4 Continue the wraps down to the bend of the hook. Then let the bobbin hang to prepare to put on the tail.

5 Select a large hackle from the upper part of the neck. Fan it to expose a number of fibers. The one shown is just about the right size for this hook.

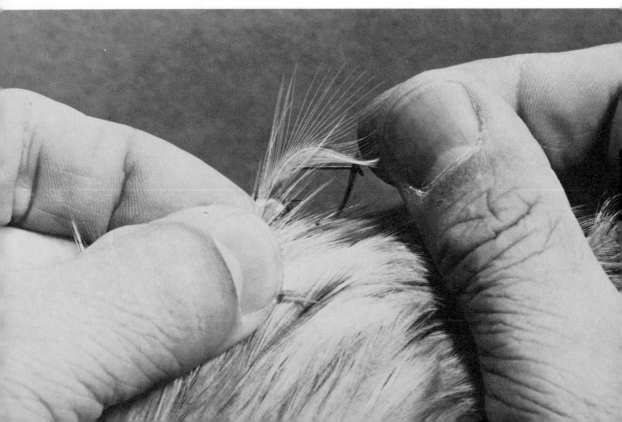

6 Tear away a segment of the hackle fibers, retaining no more than about 12–15.

7 Transfer the fibers to the right hand. If you do it carefully, the tip ends will remain properly aligned.

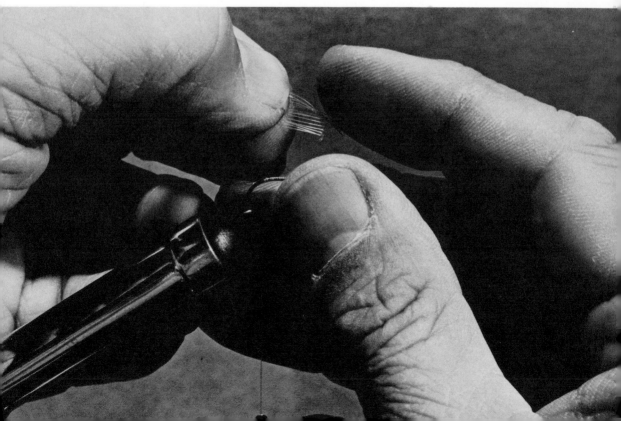

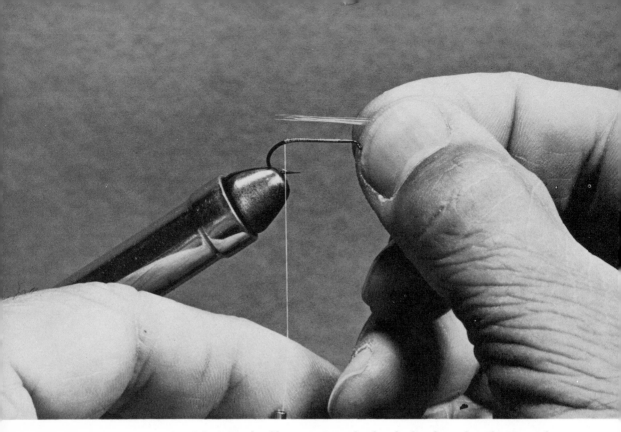

8 Measure the fibers against the hook shank so that they may be tied in to be just as long as from the bend to behind the eye.

9 Holding the fibers in the position shown, at about a 45° angle, take one turn of the thread over the fibers atop the hook shank.

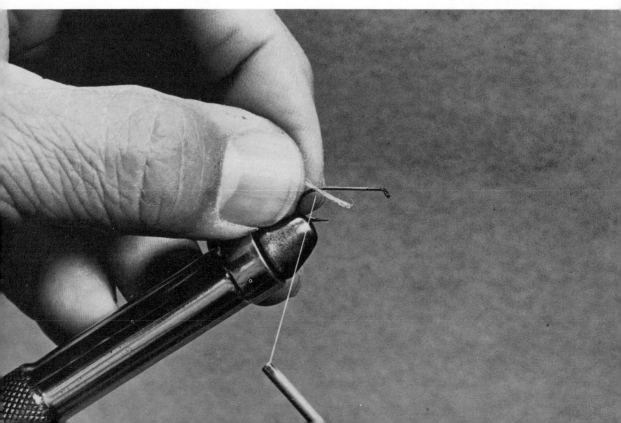

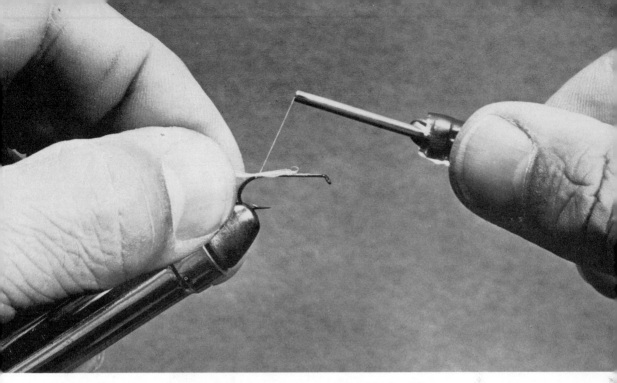

10 Take a second turn, at the same time positioning the fibers to be straight along the hook shank. If the second turn has been taken just ahead of and close to the first turn, all of the fibers will be tied in atop the shank, without slipping over the sides.

11 After a few more wraps are taken, trim off the stubs and then make more turns to cover the fibers completely. Next you will wind the thread back to the bend of the hook in preparation to winding on a prepared body. At this stage, you can put some head cement on the thread-wrapped hook shank to cement in position the materials to come.

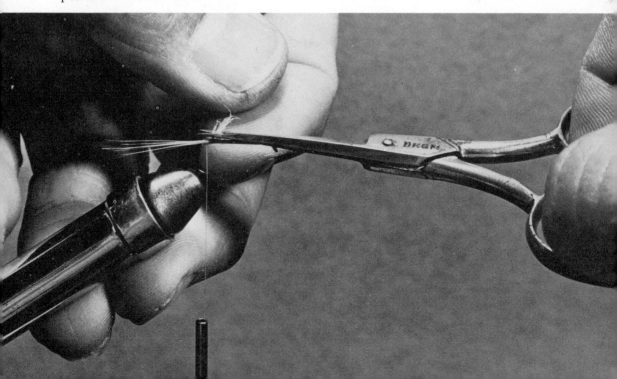

PROCEDURE 2: TYING ON WING MATERIALS

Wings for Wet Flies This procedure applies to any act of tying feathers or hair on top of the hook and is another way of tying in the tail, described above.

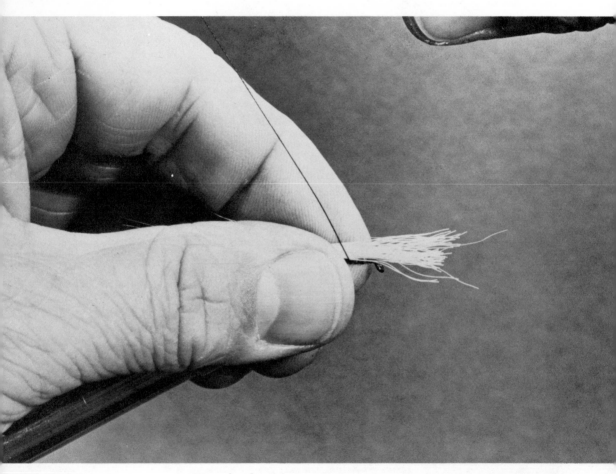

1 Here, bucktail hairs are laid along the hook shank and held on top with the thumb and forefinger, allowing no slippage of the hairs down over either side. Bring the thread up and over to the left while opening the thumb and forefinger slightly. Hold the thread in a vertical position fairly taut and close the thumb and forefinger over the thread.

2 Pull the thread down over the other side of the hook, loosening the forefinger slightly to allow the thread to slip in along the far side of the hook shank.

3 When the thread has been positioned on the other side of the hook, opposite the first strand of thread, pinch the hairs tightly and using several tugs, pull down on the bobbin to tighten the thread over the hairs. As you can see, if the thumb and forefinger have held all materials tightly enough, the thread will tie the hairs into position atop the hook as desired.

4 Make one more turn of the thread the same way, and then release the fingers and inspect the results. If any of the hair has slipped down over either side, your fingers may have slipped. Practice the operation until you can do it properly.

5 Make a number of turns forward of the first two turns to secure the wing. These turns *must* be made *in front* of the original two wraps, or the thread will begin to pull the hairs down along the sides of the hook shank. After completing the securing turns, the stubs of the hairs may be cut off and wrapped with thread.

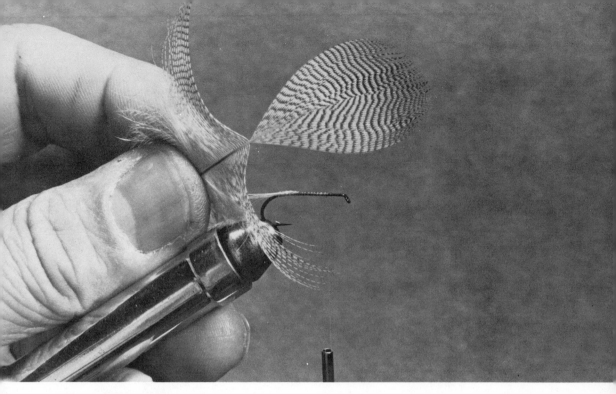

Wings for Dry Flies

1   Select a wood-duck flank feather (or suitably dyed imitation) which has come from a mature bird, choosing one which has its fibers evenly distributed on both sides of the stem. Note that the fibers do not adhere one to another on the lower part of the feather. Pull these fibers down, and then remove them or hold them back out of the way.

2   Approximately halfway up the portion of the stem that still has fibers, insert the scissors points and cut stem, leaving a V-shaped cut.

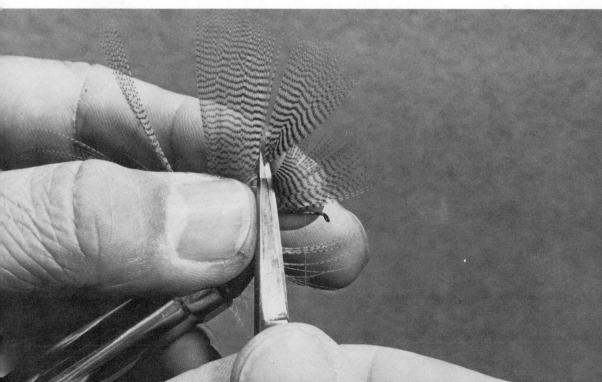

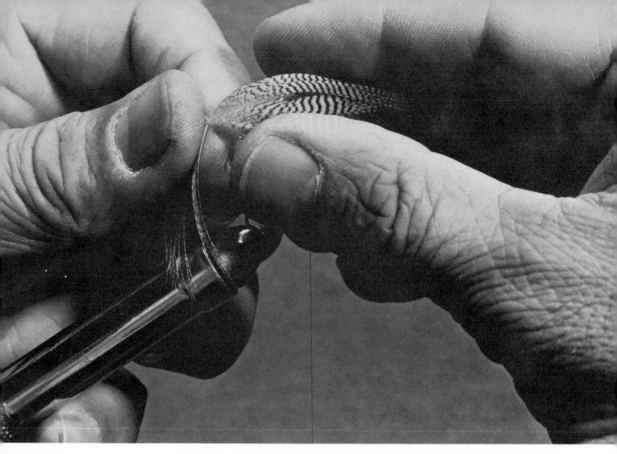

34 | **3 & 4** Holding the stem in the left hand, use the thumb and forefinger of the right hand to stroke down the two sides of the feather and bring the two back sides of the feather together.

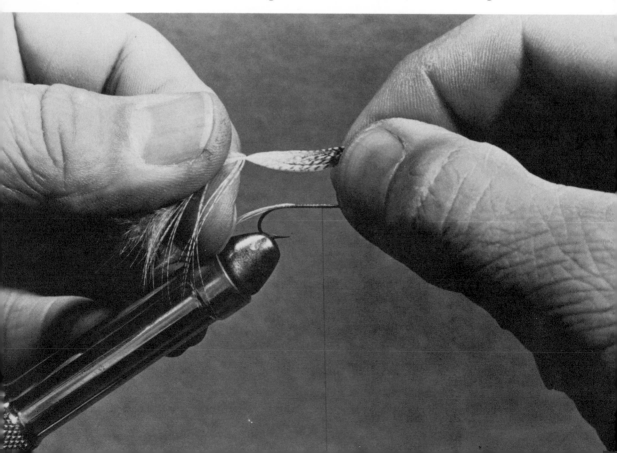

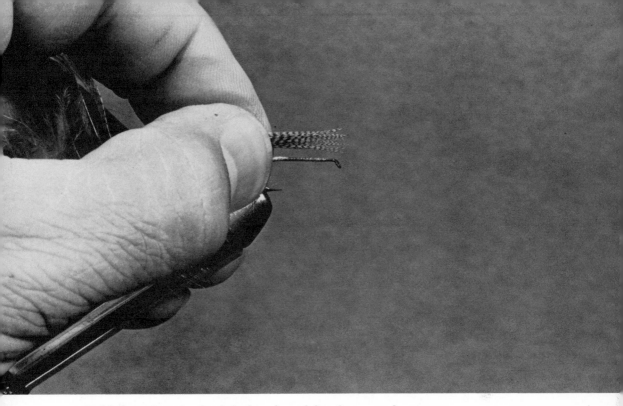

5 Hold the wings in the left thumb and forefinger and measure along the top of the hook. The wings should be as long as the distance from the eye of the hook to the rearmost curve of the bend.

6 Then move the wings toward the eye, to the position shown, and tie them in. Pinch the wings tightly, following the same procedure as in tying in bucktail for a wet fly, explained previously.

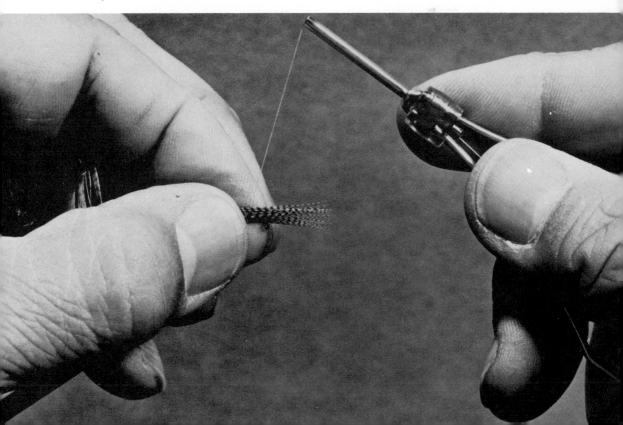

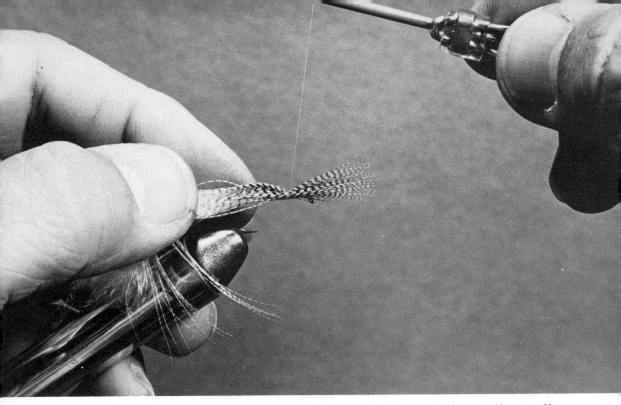

7 If Step 6 has been done correctly, the wing fibers will now all be on top of the hook shank, and none will have been pulled over to either side. Cut off the butt end of the feather and wind the thread back over the stub, tying all down completely.

8 Grasp the fibers with the left thumb and forefinger and pull back, beyond the vertical position, and make numerous turns of the tying thread to create a shoulder just in front of the fibers that will prop them in a vertical position.

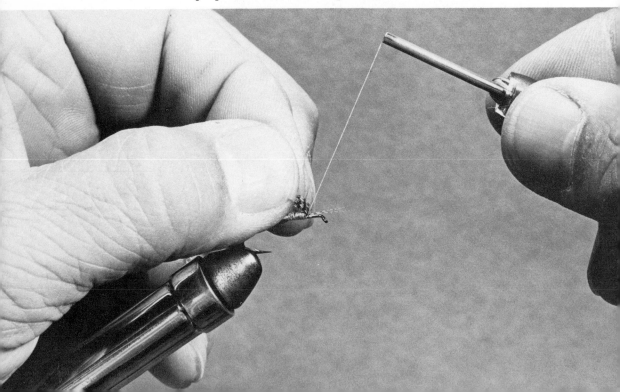

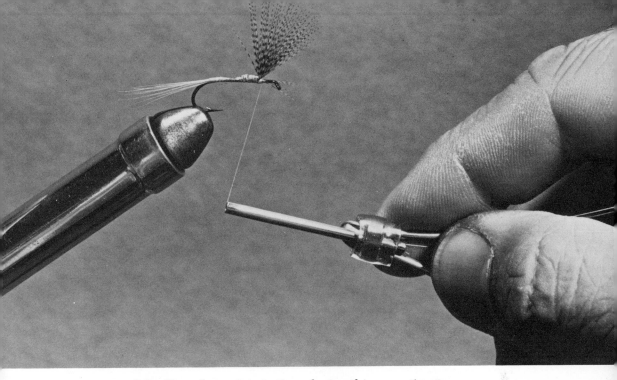

9 Let go of the fibers from time to time during this operation to see if they are in an upright position. If they aren't yet, make more turns tightly up against the fibers until they are. Then use the dubbing needle to separate the fibers evenly for the individual wings.

10 Grasp the wing on the far side and run the thread from the rear into the space between the wings, as shown. Then grasp the closer wing and run the thread from the front into that same space. This is commonly referred to as making a figure-8. That is what we will call the operation in subsequent instructions.

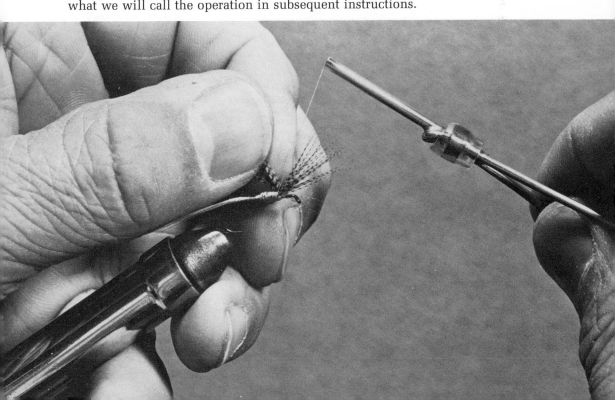

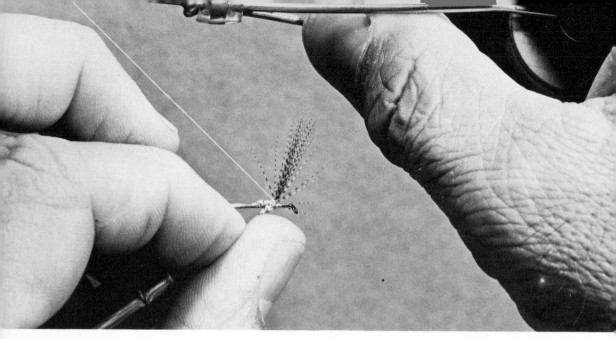

11 Repeat this figure-8 once or twice if the wings are not in an upright V and completely separated. Ordinarily, the wings can be positioned at the correct angle by the figure-8 method. But feathers do not always act according to plan. If the wings aren't properly angled, make a turn of the thread around the base of the stubborn wing (or wings) in a clockwise direction for the near wing and counterclockwise direction for the far wing, returning the thread to behind the wing to pull it back, or in front of the wing to pull it forward. The thread is then run over the hook shank away from the wing being anchored. If you have to anchor the left wing with this procedure, the thread will end up wrapped on the hook in the wrong direction. This can be easily rectified by a simple half-turn around the base of the wings, returning the thread to the "over and away" direction.

12 The completed wings, clearly separated and upright.

PROCEDURE 3: THE WHIP FINISH

The whip finish is used to make a neat, tight final fastening after all the materials for a fly have been tied in and the head has been completed. For clarity in the photographs here, a whip finish is made on a bare hook.

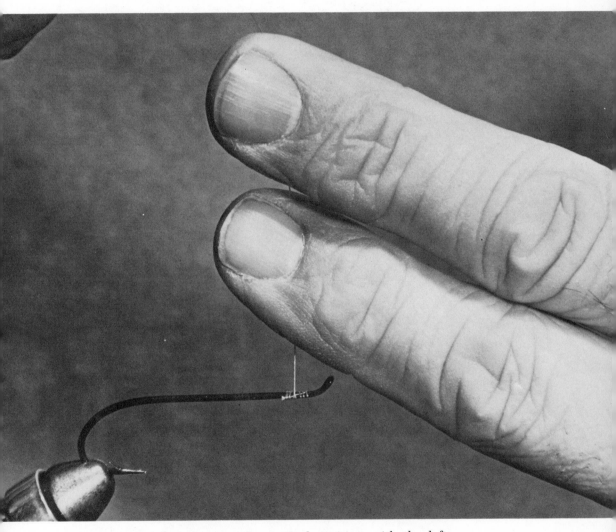

1 Bring tying thread up to the vertical position with the left hand. Position right hand with palm outward and place two fingers against thread.

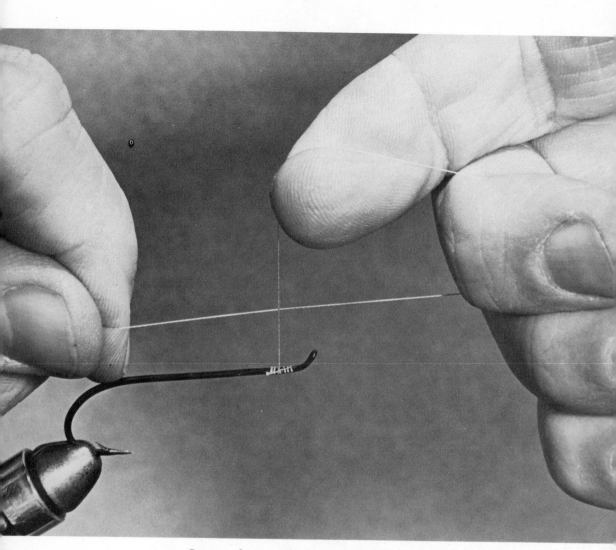

2 Create a loop with the two fingers by rotating right hand till palm faces the body. Lower the left hand during this operation to bring the thread to position shown. The strand being held in the left hand should now be horizontal and on the other side of the vertical strand. Hold all tautly.

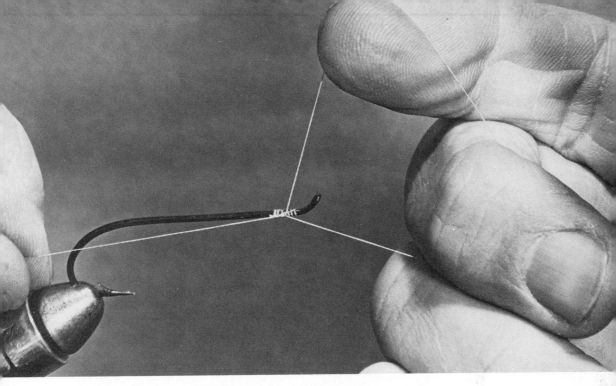

3 Lower the thread being held in the left hand into gap where vertical thread joins the hook shank, to trap the horizontal thread there. Catch the horizontal thread against the hook by moving the right hand away from the body.

4 Release the horizontal thread and let it hang, and grasp the vertical strand of the loop with the left hand. Keep this vertical strand taut so it will continue to hold the horizontal strand in its position.

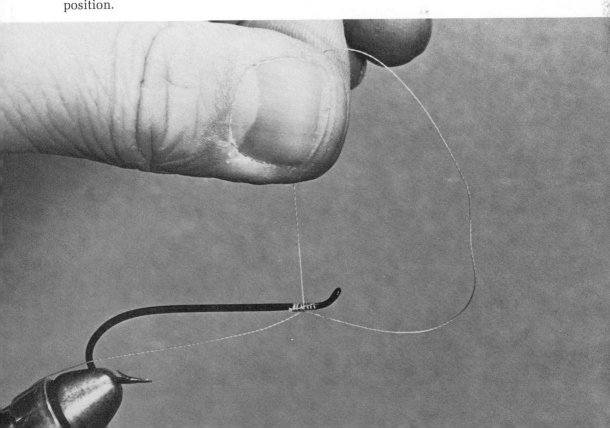

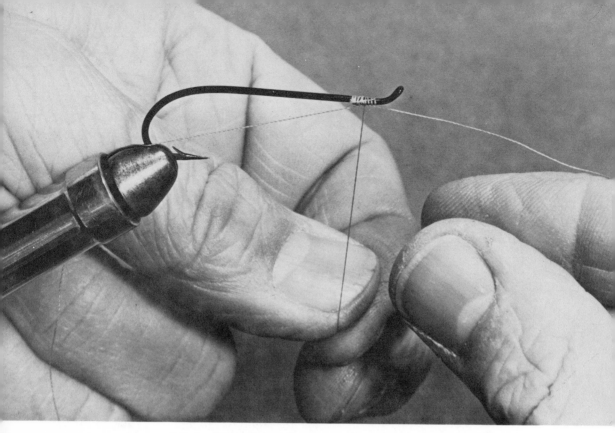

5 & 6 Wrap the vertical strand on the hook at least three or four times, being careful not to disrupt the loop previously formed. Pass the thread from left to right hands and back to make the wraps, always maintaining tension.

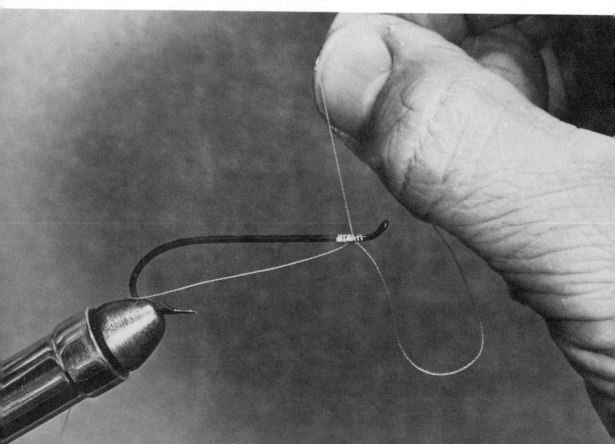

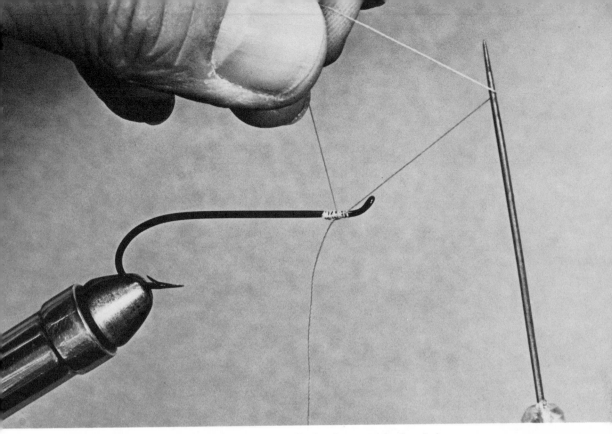

7 & 8 After completing the turns, catch the loop with the dubbing needle. Hold the loop taut with the needle, let go of it with the left hand, grasp the left end of the horizontal strand, and pull it to close the loop.

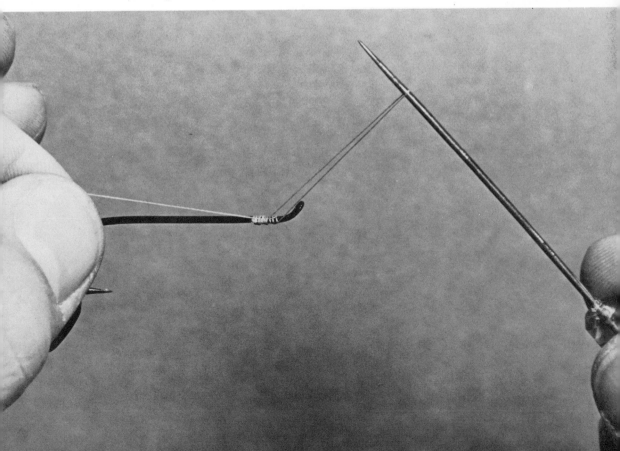

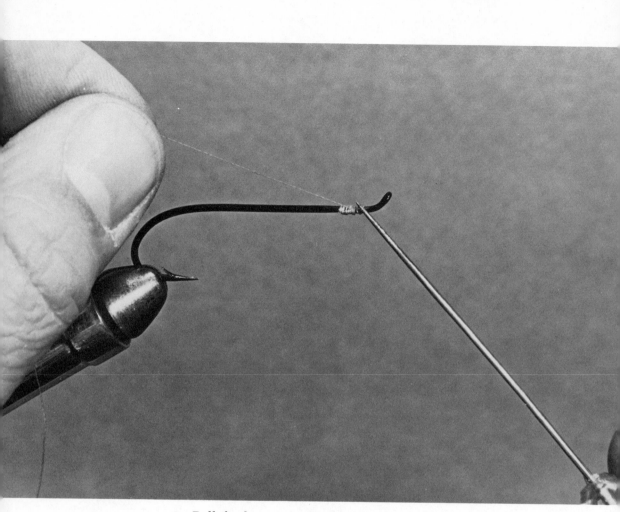

9 Pull the loop completely closed and remove the needle, and the whip finish is complete. Cut off the remaining thread.

5
Bucktails and Streamers

BUCKTAILS AND STREAMERS ARE BOTH INTENDED TO IMITATE OR represent small baitfish rather than "flies." The principal difference between them is that bucktails are made with hair wings and streamers are made with feather wings. This chapter explains how to tie one of each: the Black Nosed Dace, a bucktail, and the Black Ghost, a streamer.

BLACK NOSED DACE

Materials used

> Hook: 3X–6X long shank Limerick
> Tail: red wool yarn
> Body: silver tinsel, medium width
> Wing: bucktail, brown over black over white

1   After tying on thread and covering hook shank (Procedure 1), select a 3-inch piece of red wool yarn and tie it in on top of hook at the bend to make a tail 1/2 inch in length. Then carefully place the remainder of the yarn along the top of the hook and wrap the tying thread lightly over it, moving toward the eye and holding the yarn in position with the fingers. The yarn will then be evenly laid along the hook. Make another wrapping of thread to the tail and then still another back to the eye. This will create a thickened base for the tinsel body. Trim the excess yarn as shown.

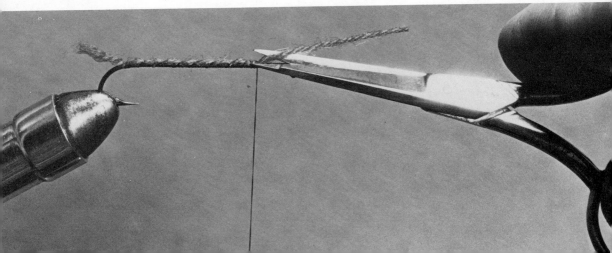

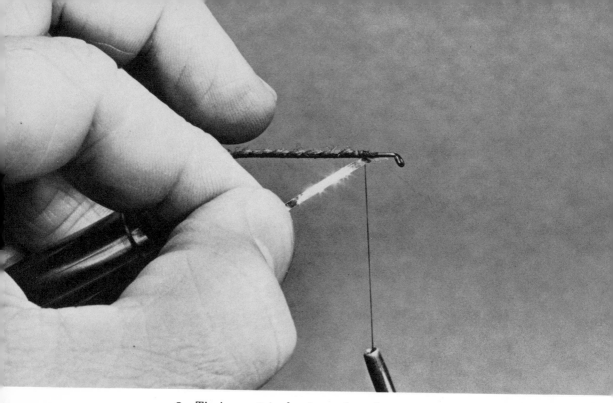

2 Tie in an 8-inch piece of medium-width silver tinsel under the hook shank about 1/4 inch behind the eye, preparatory to wrapping.

3 Wrap the tinsel toward the rear of the hook. Use the right hand for the up-and-over wrap, then exchange to the left hand to come beyond and below the hook. Take care to avoid any gaps between the winds, but don't overlap.

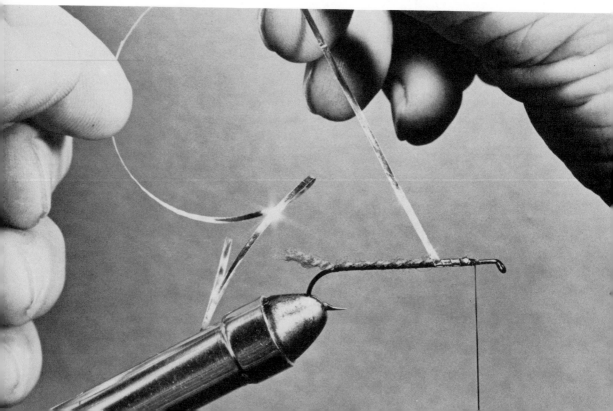

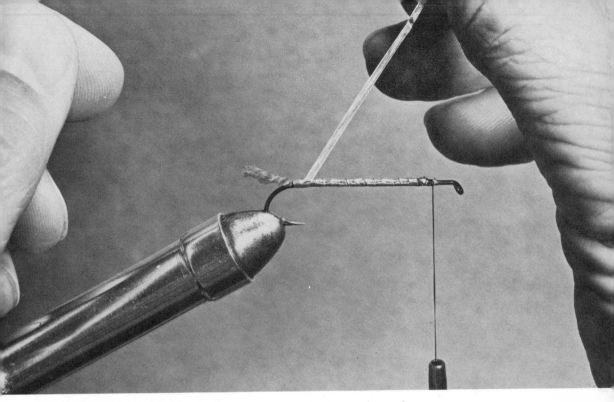

4 When you reach the hook bend, reverse direction and wrap back to the point where the tinsel was originally tied in.

5 Grasp the tinsel with the right hand, hold it out to the right, and make three turns with the tying thread to fasten the tinsel tightly in place. Cut the tinsel close to the hook and make four more turns to tie down the stub.

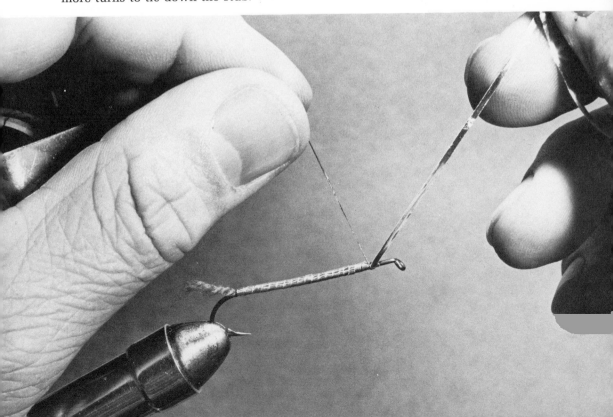

6 Cut a bunch of white hair from a bucktail, choosing the hairs nearest the tip of the tail, as they are the best quality. Even up the tip ends of the hairs before tying in. (A good way to do this is to put the tips in a cylindrical lipstick cover and tap it on the tabletop.)

7 Tie in white bucktail, using Procedure 2, positioning it so that a third of the length of the hair extends beyond the rear of the tinsel body.

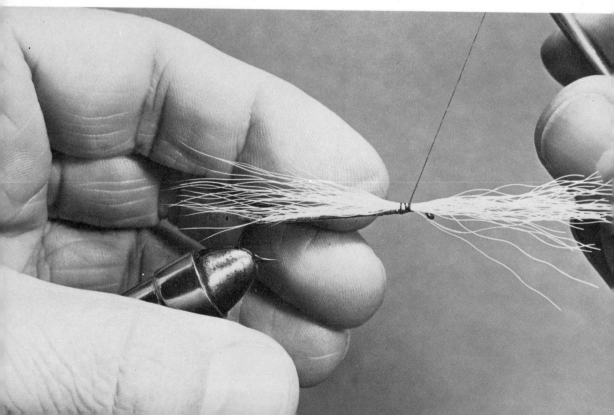

8 Using the same procedure, tie in a smaller bunch of black bucktail (found in the center of your "white" bucktail), on top of the white bucktail.

9 The length of this part of the wing should be slightly shorter than the lower wing.

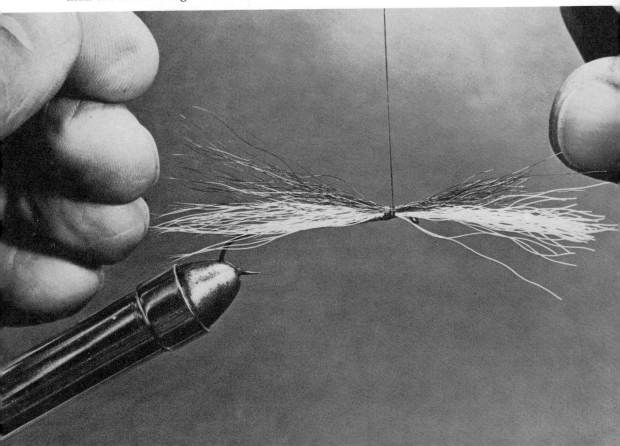

10 Repeat this operation with brown bucktail hairs, putting them atop the black wing. This segment of the wing should be the same length as the lowest (white) part of the wing. Then cut off all of the stubs of hair protruding beyond the hook eye, holding the scissors at an angle and slanting up and toward the rear of the fly. This will facilitate the wrapping of the tapered head which is desirable on all your flies.

11 Make numerous wraps of thread over the hair stubs, taking care to build up a tapered head in so doing. Complete with whip finish (Procedure 3) and apply head cement in small droplets with bodkin point to all sides of the head.

BLACK GHOST

Materials used

Hook: 3X–6X long shank Limerick
Tail: yellow hackle fibers
Body: black wool yarn with medium width
  silver tinsel rib
Beard: yellow hackle fibers
Wing: four white saddle hackles
Shoulder: two jungle-cock nails (or suitable imitation)

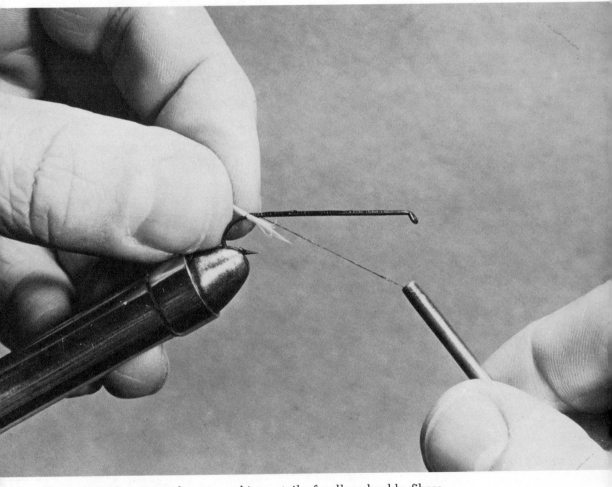

1 Complete Procedure 1, making a tail of yellow hackle fibers
1/2 inch long.

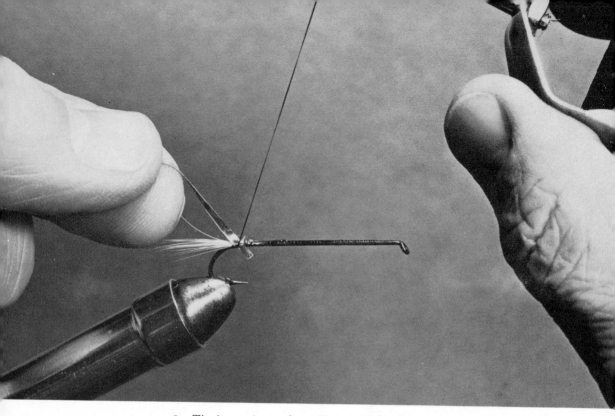

2 Tie in a piece of medium width silver tinsel about 5 inches long beneath the hook at the point where the tail has been tied in. Leave hanging.

3 Tie in 12-inch piece of black wool yarn under the hook about 1/2 inch behind the eye.

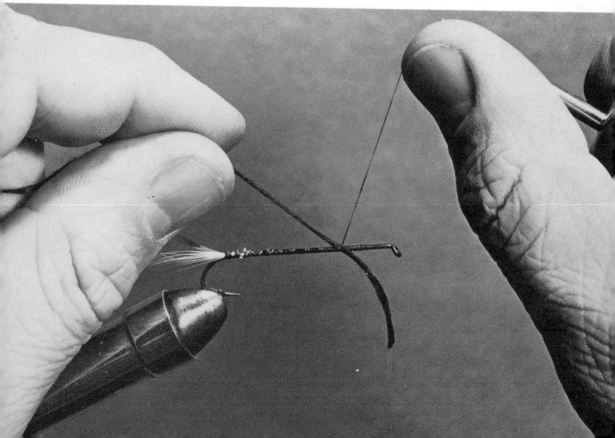

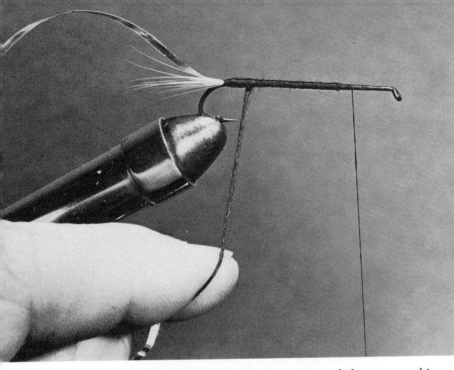

4 Begin the tapered body by wrapping toward the rear, making close turns on the front half and looser turns toward the bend of the hook. Then reverse direction, returning toward the front of the body.

5 At this point, bear in mind that the properly shaped streamer body should be heavier in the fore part, tapering to the rear. This is controlled by making more turns over one another as you move toward the front of the body. Control this by visual inspection during this whole operation.

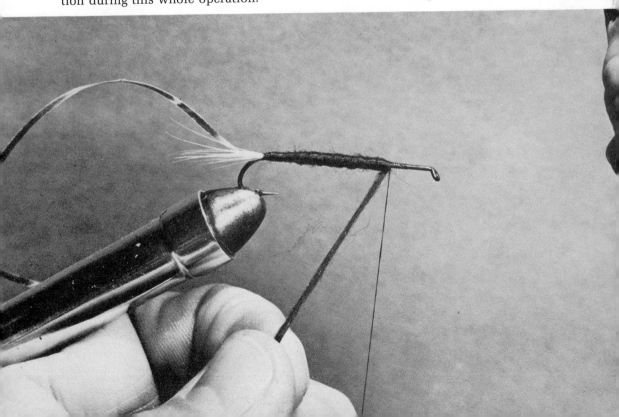

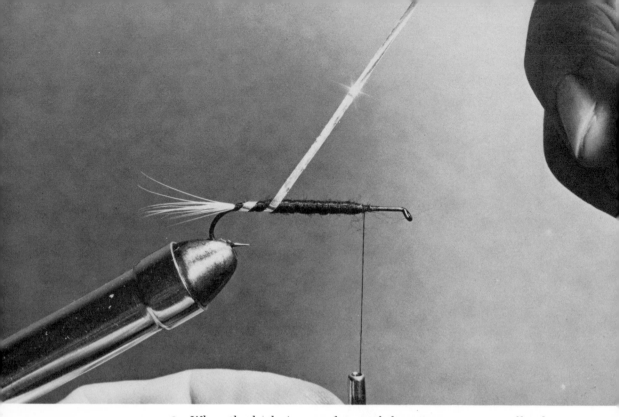

6 When the body is complete and the excess yarn cut off, take up the silver tinsel which has been left hanging and wrap it toward the eye, leaving a gap between winds as shown.

7 When you have wound all the way forward on body, creating a widely separated silver rib, tie off the tinsel and cut off the excess.

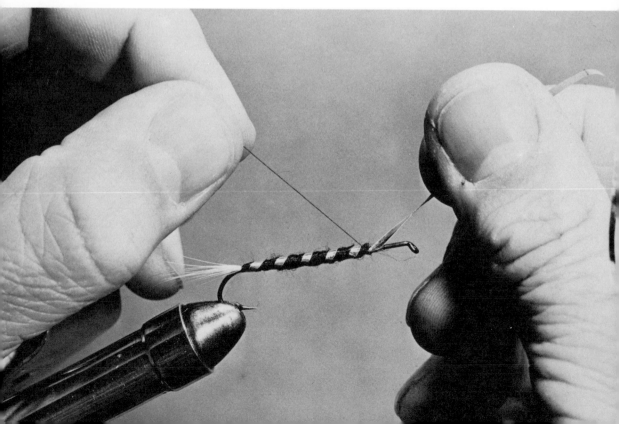

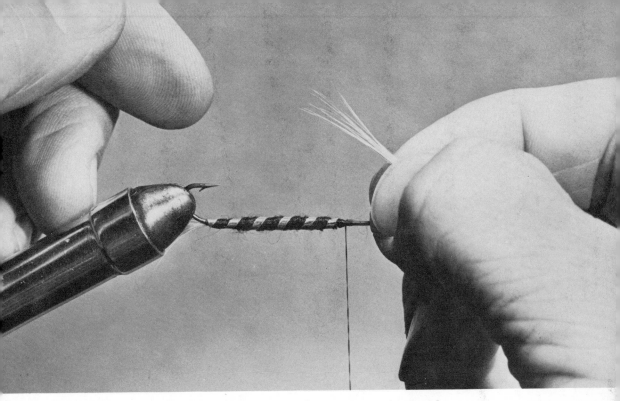

8 Remove the fly from the vise and reposition it upside down. Select about 12 yellow hackle fibers the same length as the tail.

9 Tie in the hackle fibers at the front of the body, using Procedure 2. If these are tied in close to the front of the body, the body's bulge will cause the fibers to be propped up at an angle as shown. Make further wraps of the thread toward the eye to tie in securely.

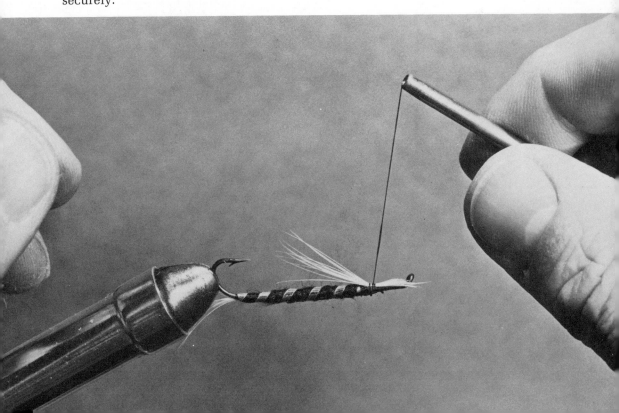

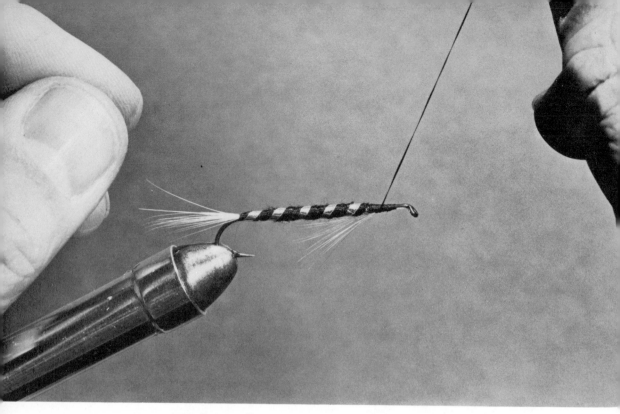

10 Return fly to its original position and make more turns of thread over the yellow hackle to create an even base for the next operation.

11 Select four white saddle hackles of uniform shape and strip the fibers from the lower portion of the stems, leaving enough for the desired length, as shown here. About a third of the wing should extend beyond the rear of the body.

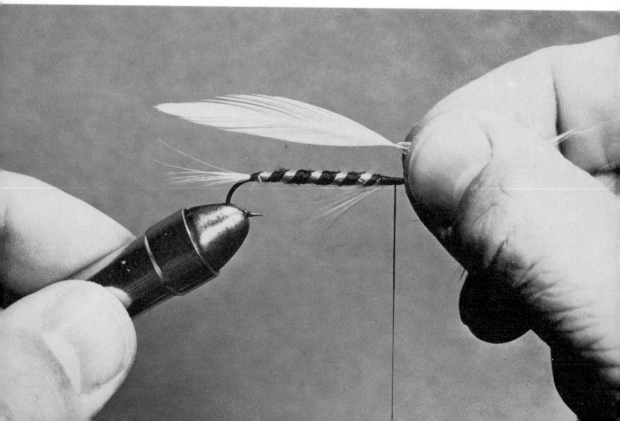

12 Arrange the four hackle feathers so that the two on each side can be placed on the fly with the good sides facing outward. The result will be that each pair is positioned on the back of the fly with a possible outward bow, and the tips of the pairs will touch at the rear. Hold firmly in this position with the fingers and proceed to fasten to the top of the hook, following Procedure 2.

13 The next material to be added is the jungle-cock eyes (or nails). Two eyes must be selected for uniformity from a jungle-cock neck.

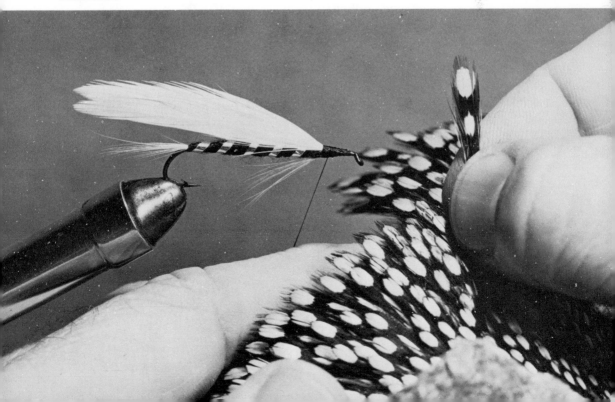

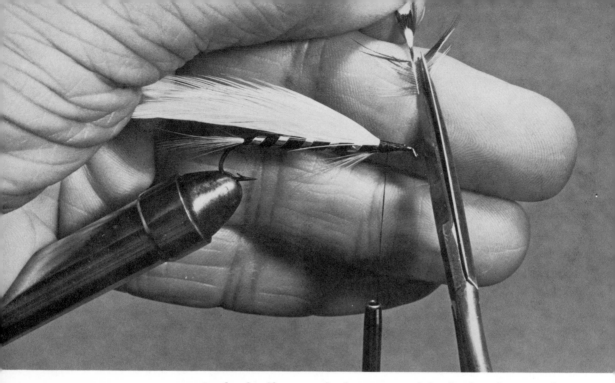

14 Stroke the fibers on the lower part of the feather downward and with the scissors carefully trim them away close to the stem, leaving very short stubs on each side. The stubs will facilitate proper positioning alongside the hook shank when tying in.

15 Position the right eye as shown. Hold it in place with the left thumb, and make a few light turns of thread to hold in position. The next wraps can be made more tightly, to complete the installation of this eye. In the same way, tie in the other eye on the opposite side of the fly. Complete the fly with the whip finish and apply head cement.

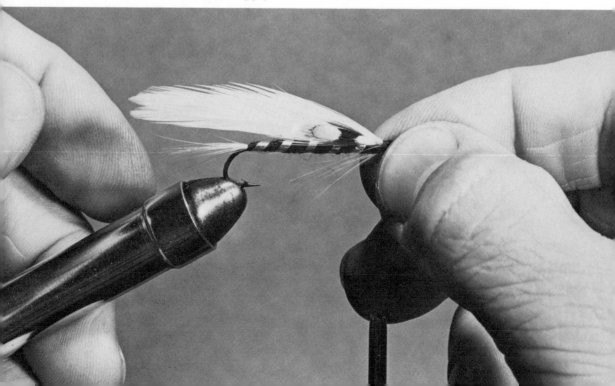

6
Wet Flies

THE WET FLY IS DIFFERENT THINGS TO DIFFERENT FISHERMEN, and even today there is no consensus as to what the trout thinks. After all, this is the most important point.

It was at one time exclusively considered to be an imitation of a drowned insect—one that had been riding on the surface of the water and for some reason had sunk in the moving water. Then, because the wet fly was so successfully fished on the downstream swing, thereby moving very fast across the current, there was conjecture that trout considered it not a drowned fly but a minnow, or a fast-moving nymph, or a caddis fly rising to the surface, etc.

Actually, the construction of the wet fly does not constitute an imitation of an insect, so the only conclusion I can come to is that it does create the impression of some form of underwater life to a hungry trout, by its movement and appearance.

Most important, wet flies are fish-getters, and among the many patterns in existence, I was pleased to conclude that the Leadwing Coachman and Dark Cahill wet flies not only are high on the list of fish-getters but also serve to illustrate the different procedures used to tie most wet flies.

DARK CAHILL

Materials used

Hook: #10 or #12 Model Perfect wet fly
Tail: wood-duck flank feather fibers
Body: gray muskrat underbody fur
Beard: brown hackle fibers
Wing: wood-duck flank feather segment

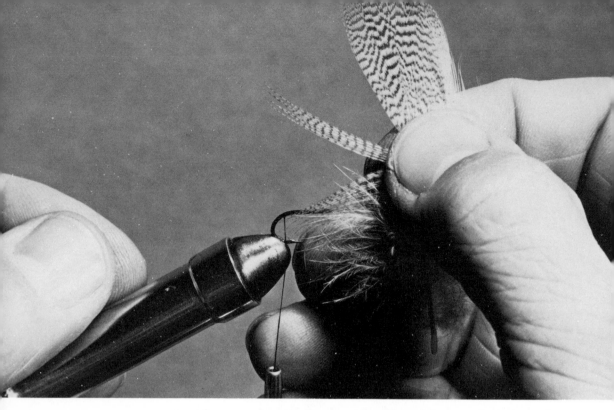

1 After covering the hook with a thread base, select a wood-duck flank feather and separate a segment of the straight fibers which will be found along the side of the feather.

2 Cut off these fibers and tie them in as a tail, which must be as long as the hook shank from behind the eye to the bend.

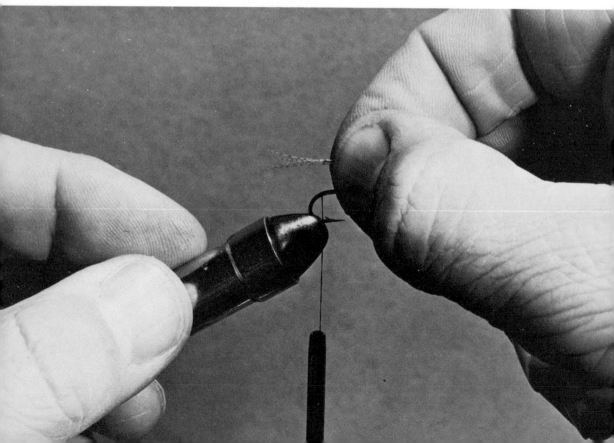

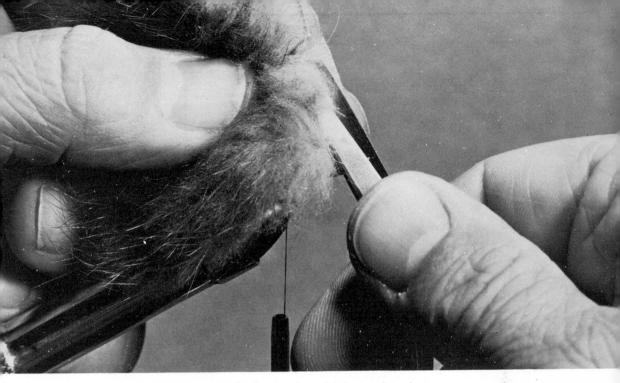

3 This fly will have a gray fur body, for which muskrat hair is used. Cut off a portion of the hair from a piece of muskrat skin, removing it close to the skin. Your heavier scissors will do the job easily.

4 Examine the hair you have removed. It will include some long heavier hairs, which will protrude for the most part. These are the guard hairs and must be removed before preparing the body.

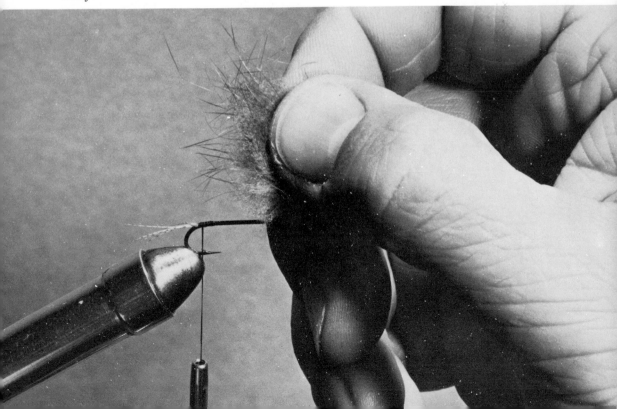

5 The residue of soft gray fur must be mixed thoroughly by pulling it apart and matting it together again a number of times until a pad of well-mixed fur has been created.

6 Take a small bit of the pad of fur and roll it onto the tying thread with thumb and forefinger. Muskrat fur spins onto the thread more easily than many dubbing materials, but a little extra wax on the thread will help it stick if you have trouble.

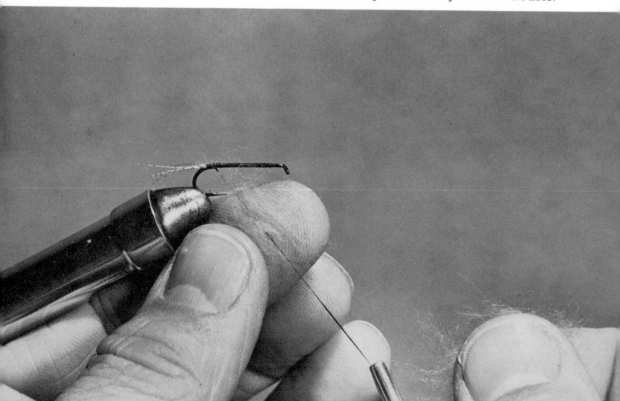

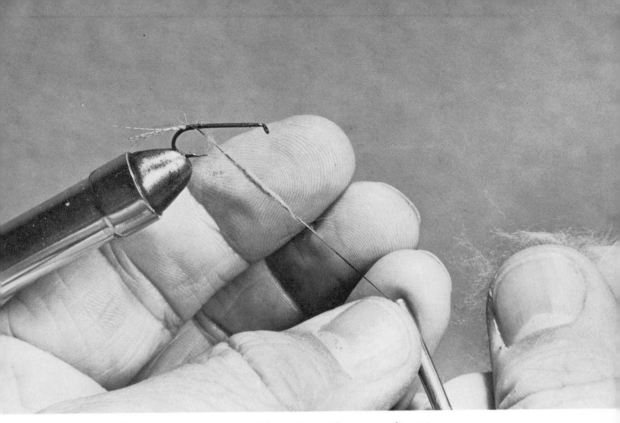

7 The rolling operation must always be in the same direction. This will be easier if you use too little rather than too much fur in applying to the thread.

8 Repeat the operation a number of times until you have a "rope" of fur 2 inches long.

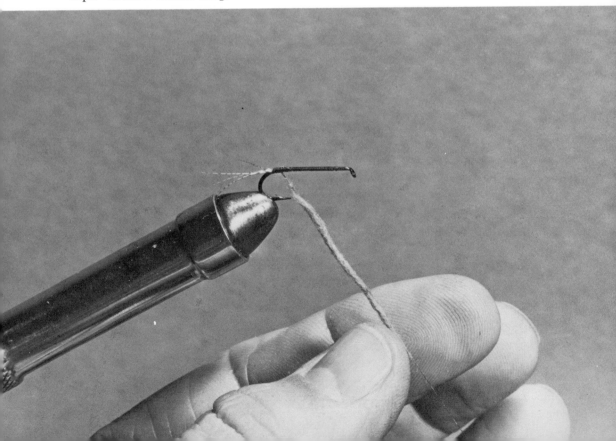

9 Wrap the fur on the hook, controlling the turns so that the body will be heavier in the front, creating a tapered body.

10 You will probably find that you do not have enough fur to wrap the whole body, so before all of the fur has been wrapped on, apply some more fur to the thread as needed to complete the body, covering three-quarters of the hook.

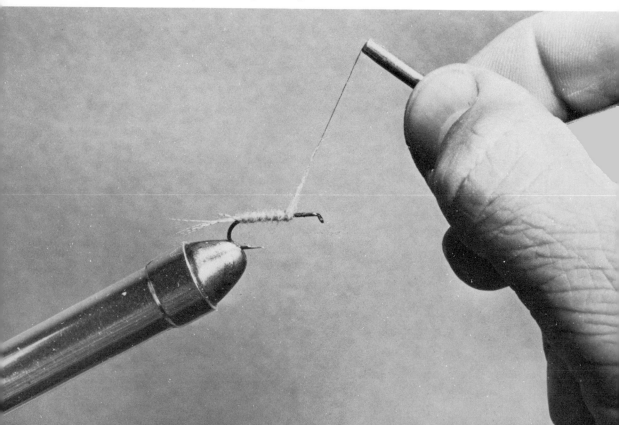

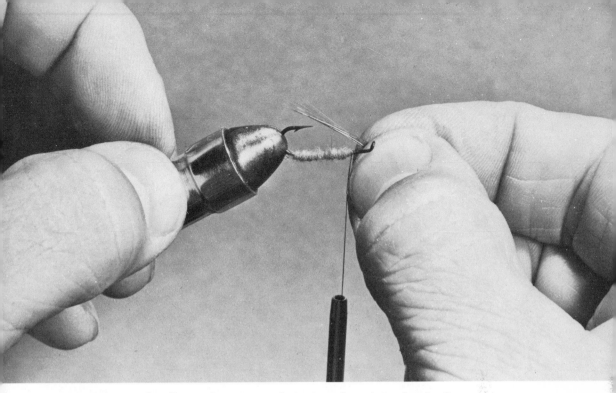

11 Reverse the fly in the vise and tie in a beard (or legs) of brown hackle fibers, following the procedure described for the Black Ghost. The length of the legs should be sufficient to reach and cover the point of the hook.

12 Reverse the fly again, to normal position. Take the wood-duck flank feather again, cut a 1/2-inch segment of the straight fibers, and roll them into a tight bunch to be tied on top of the hook.

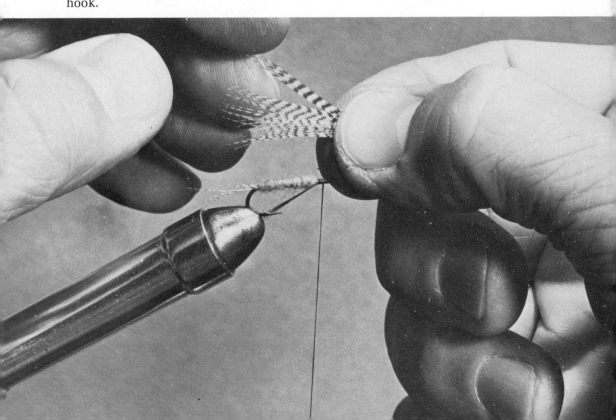

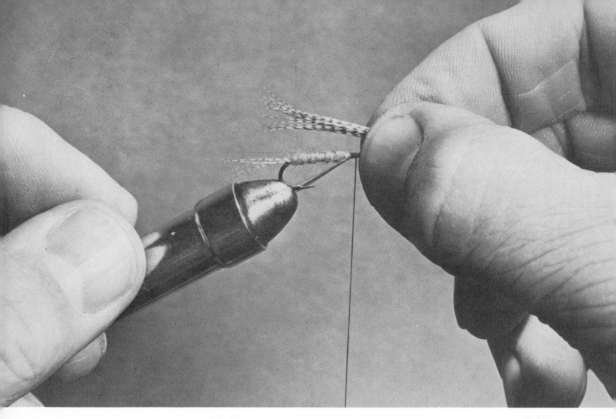

13 Hold the wings in place so that they protrude to a point midway down the tail.

14 Tie in the wings, following Procedure 2, and then cut off the excess fibers.

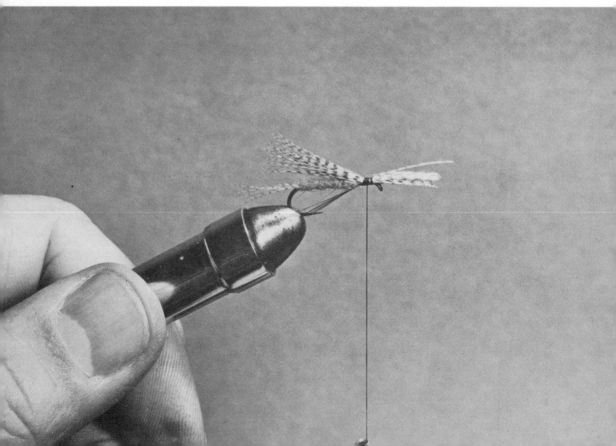

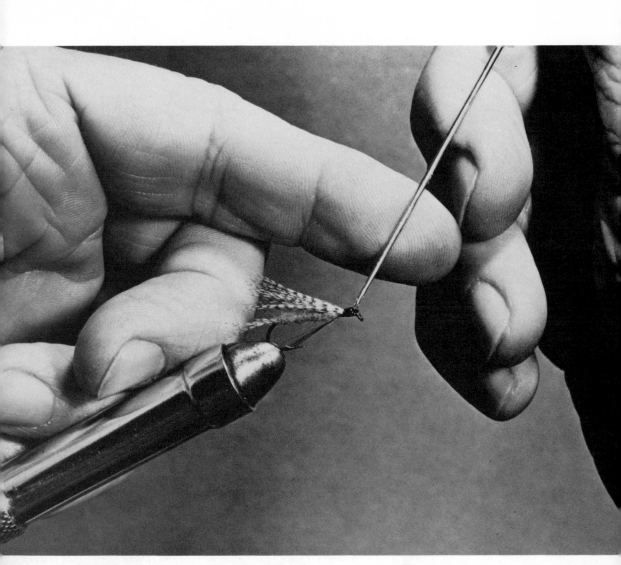

15 Complete the fly with a whip finish and apply head cement.

LEADWING COACHMAN

Materials used

    Hook: #10 or #12 Model Perfect wet fly
    Tail: none
    Tag: medium gold tinsel
    Body: six peacock herls
    Beard: brown hackle fibers
    Wing: mallard quill segments

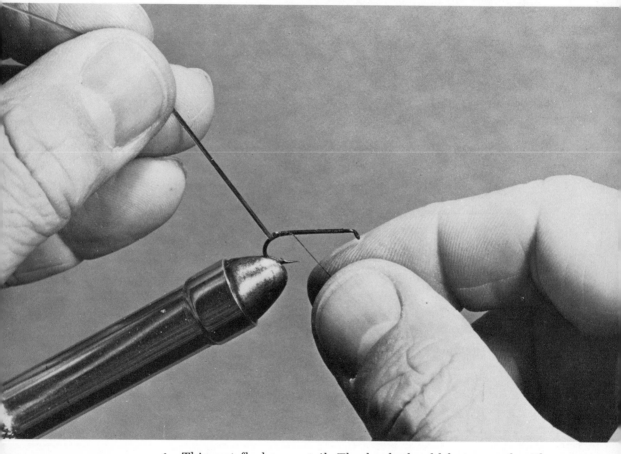

1 This wet fly has no tail. The hook should be covered with thread only, in the first operation. Just forward of the bend, about 1/8 inch, tie in a 4-inch piece of medium width gold tinsel and wrap it down over the bend of the hook for about 1/8 inch, as shown.

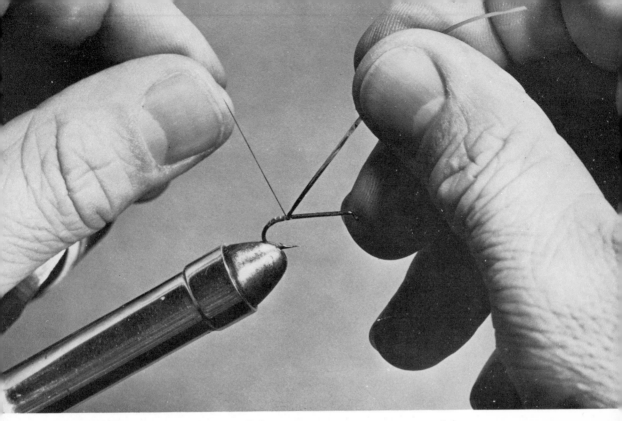

2 Wrap the tinsel back toward the eye to its starting point and tie it off. You should now have about 3/16 inch of gold wrapping, and this is known as the tag. Cut off the excess tinsel.

3 To prepare for making the herl body, make a loop of thread about 8 inches long and tie it in at the front of the tag.

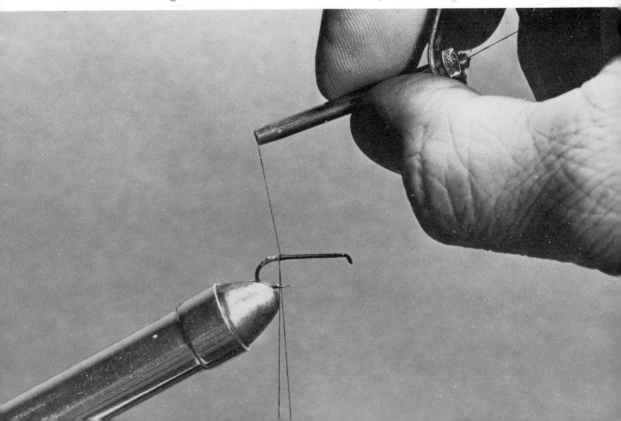

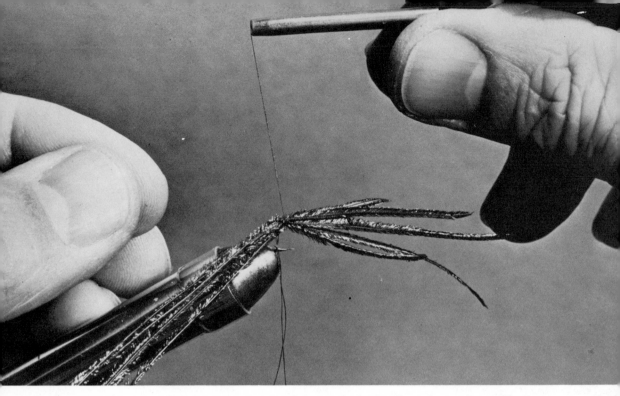

4 Select six strips of peacock herl taken from the stalk just below the eye and tie them in by the tips, beneath the hook shank. Then wrap thread forward three-quarters of the way to the eye of the hook.

5 Separate the loop of thread previously prepared, gather all of the herls together, place them inside the loop of thread, and draw all together with one strand of thread on each side of the herls.

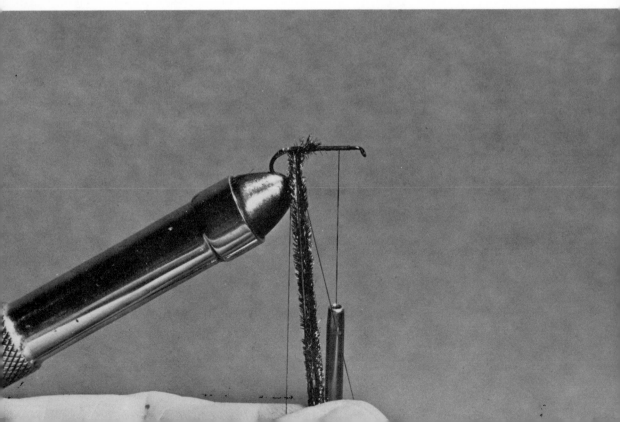

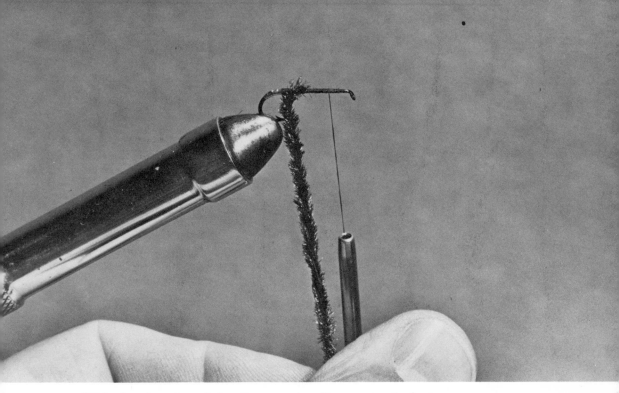

6 With the thumb and forefinger, spin all, counterclockwise, until you have created a solid fuzzy "rope."

7 Wind the spun herl forward to a point three-quarters of the way to the eye, leaving room for the wings and beard. Tie off the herl and trim the excess.

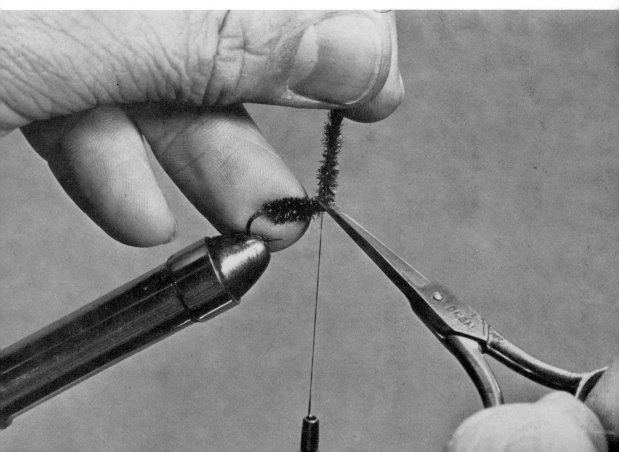

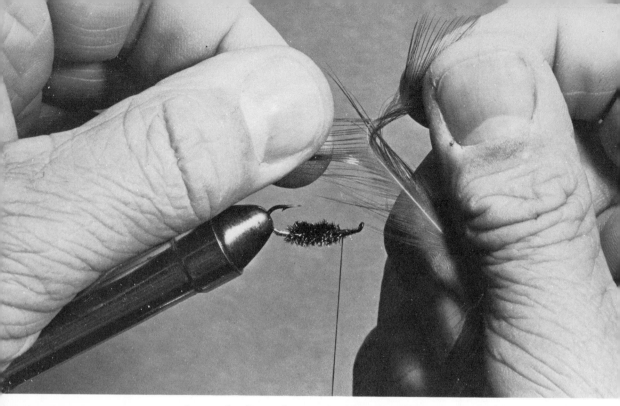

8   Invert the fly in the vise. Take a large feather from the top end of a brown neck and remove about 12 of the fibers of sufficient length to exceed the length of the hook.

9   Following Procedure 2, as used for wings, tie in the brown fibers at an angle to assure that the tips cover the hook point.

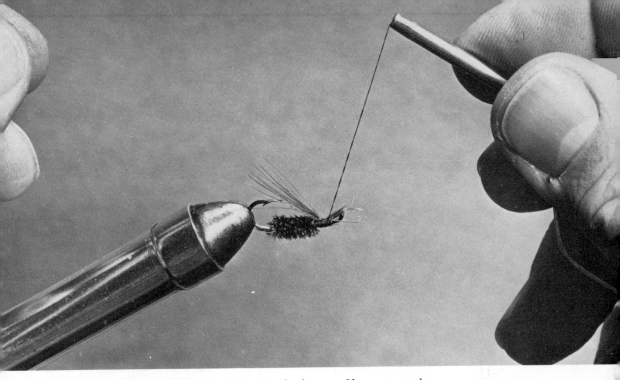

10 The front of the body should prop the brown fibers up at the desired angle. If not, take a turn or two around the wing, pull forward, then wrap thread in front.

11 Return the fly to the upright position and select two mallard primary feathers (from the leading edge of the wing), one right and one left side, as shown. These feathers are purchased in pairs as pictured or in the whole wing form. Cut a 3/16-inch-wide segment out of each feather.

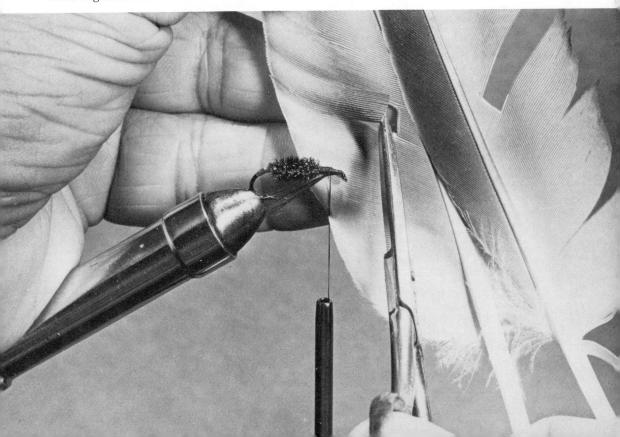

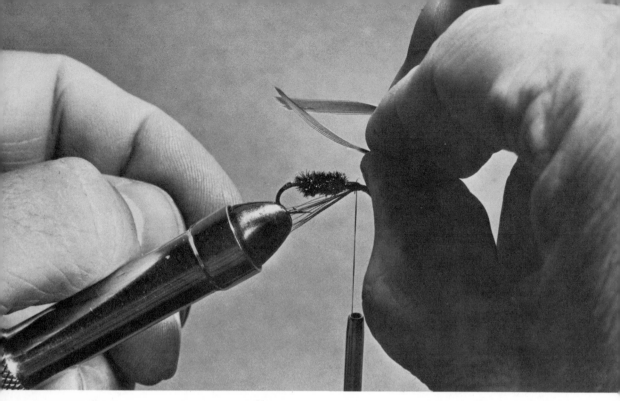

12 Position segments together so that the concave or good sides of the segments face each other. Make sure that the tips match evenly, points up.

13 Position the wings on the hook so that the tips are even with the rear of the hook.

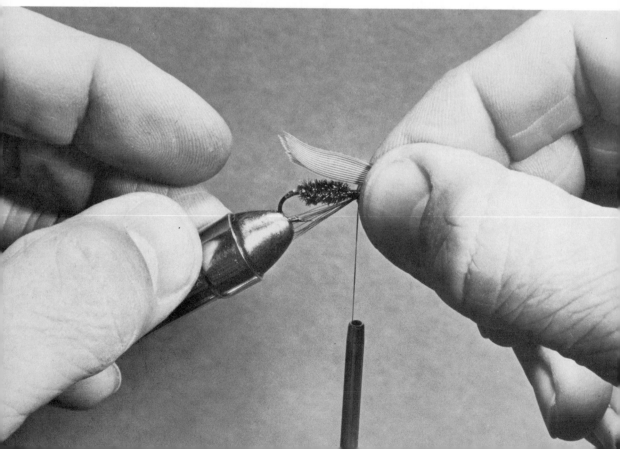

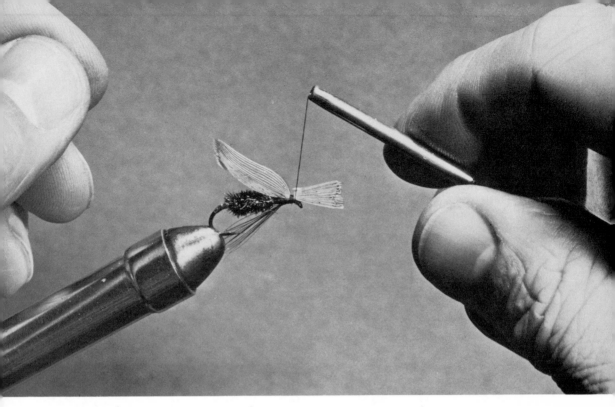

14 Tie in the wings, using Procedure 2.

15 Cut off the remaining stubs and wrap the head with enough turns to create a tapered head. Do not wind back over the wings, as this will disturb their position.

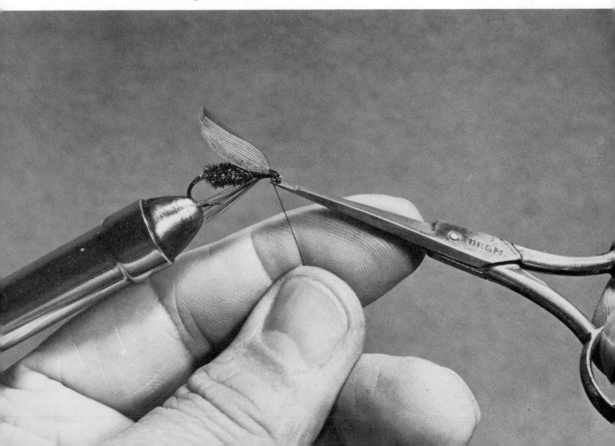

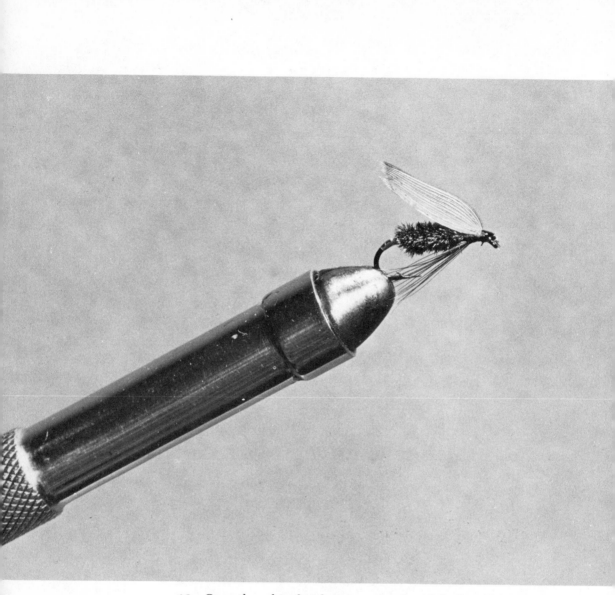

16 Once the whip finish is completed and the head cement has been applied, the fly is finished.

7
Dry Flies

DRY FLIES ARE IMITATIONS OF ADULT AQUATIC INSECTS THAT have just hatched at the surface of the water or have alit on the water, or of terrestrial insects such as ants that have fallen in the water. The natural insects hit the surface with great delicacy, and float on top of the surface film rather than actually in the water. Thus the imitations must be very light and delicate, and the hackle particularly must be of first quality. Seven good patterns are explained in this chapter. If you learn to tie these, you will know how to tie 98 percent of all dry-fly patterns in use today.

BROWN BIVISIBLE

Materials used

> Hook: #10 to #14 Model Perfect dry fly
> Tail: brown hackle fibers
> Body: brown hackle, palmered; white hackle
>   collar in front
> Wing: none

The procedure shown here for tying this fly is not the classic one, which calls for hackle to be tied in by the tip end and wound on. The problems encountered with the twisting hackle stem in the wrapping can be frustrating. The following simplified version will result in a fly which will serve the fisherman just as well on the stream, and it is infinitely easier to tie.

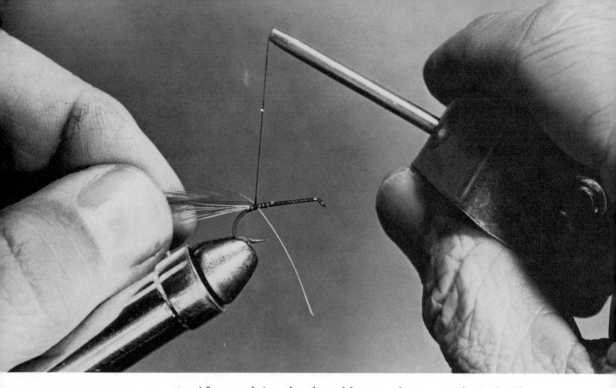

1   After applying the thread base and tying in the tail of brown hackle fibers (Procedure 1), select two brown hackles, one larger than the other, the largest to be of normal size for the fly to be tied. Remove the fibers on the lower third of each. Tie in the smallest hackle at bend of hook.

2   Wrap the hackle on to the point where the hackle fibers diminish in length and tie off. All wraps are to be close.

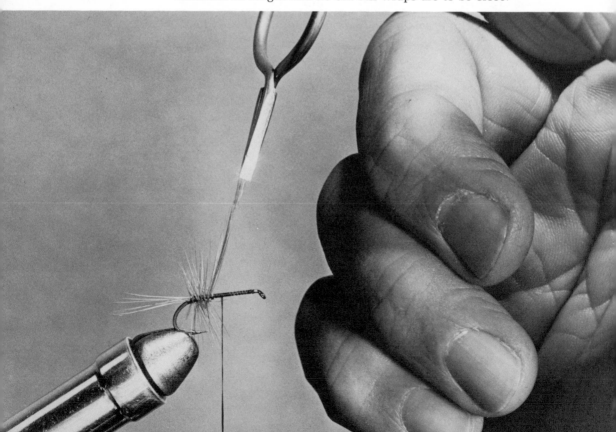

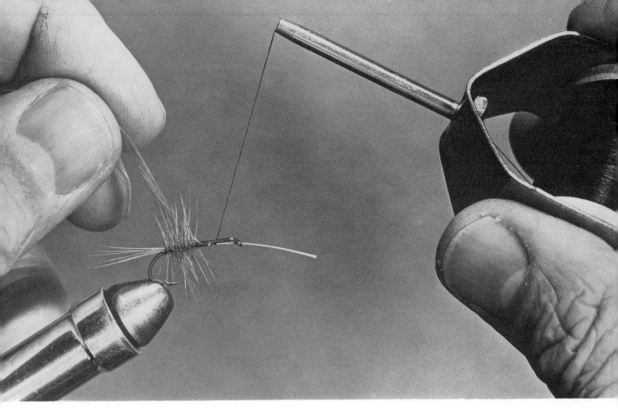

3 Tie in the larger hackle close to the previous wraps.

4 Wrap the second hackle forward, still avoiding any gaps.

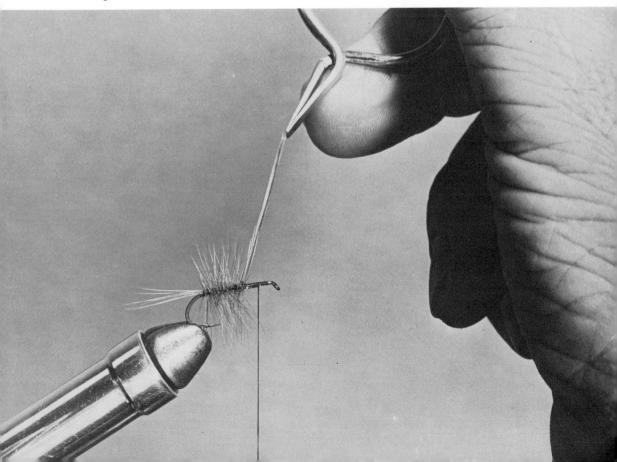

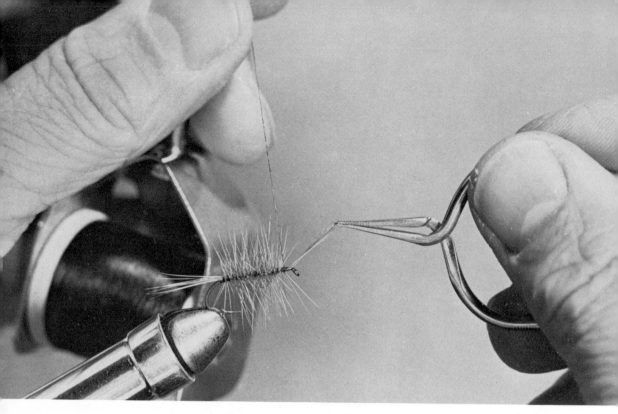

5 Tie off the second hackle, leaving a little space in which to tie in the collar. You have now completed "palmer" hackling.

6 Select a white hackle appropriate for the size of the fly and tie it in at front.

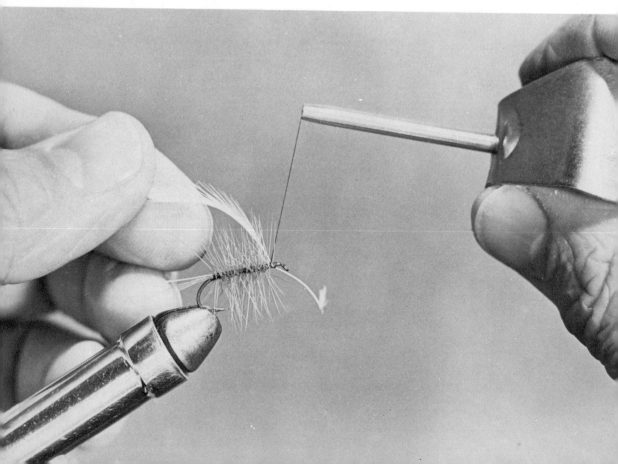

7 Take two turns of the white hackle and tie it off.

8 Complete whip finish and coat with head cement. It can now be seen why this fly is called a bivisible, with the two contrasting hackle colors clearly visible.

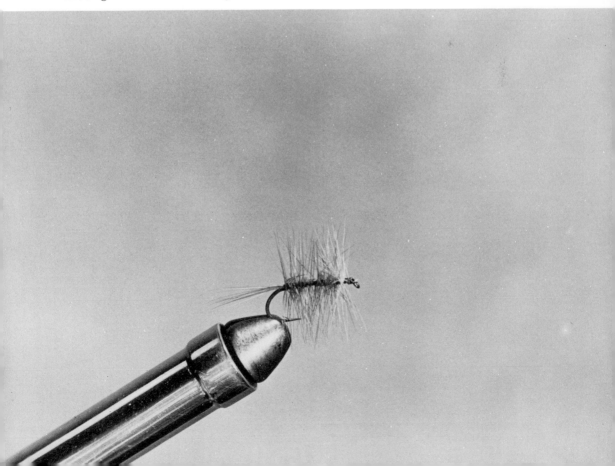

QUILL GORDON

Materials used

Hook: #10 to #18 Model Perfect dry fly
Tail: dun hackle fibers
Body: stripped peacock quill
Wing: wood-duck flank feather
Hackle: dark dun

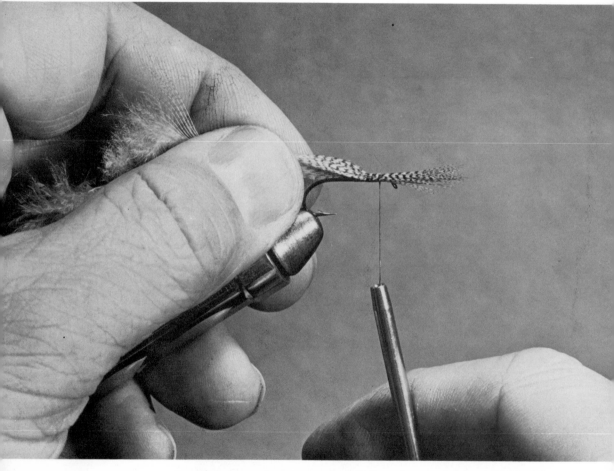

1 After wrapping a covering of thread over the front half of the hook to serve as a base on which to tie the wings, follow Procedure 2 to make a dry-fly wing from a wood-duck flank feather.

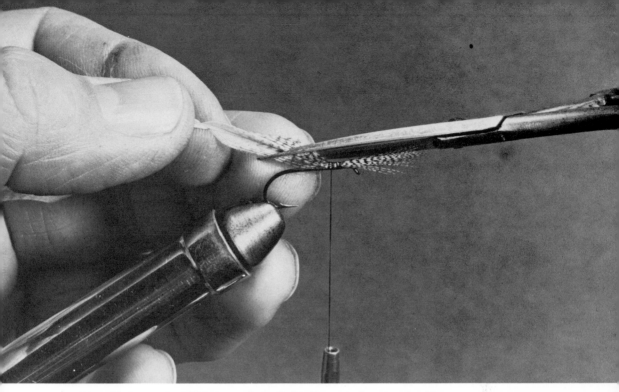

2 Cut off the stubs of the wood-duck feather as shown, at a flat angle, to leave a tapered remainder of the feather. Then tie this down completely with the thread, along the top of the hook. This creates an enlarged diameter on which to wrap the quill and will result in a tapered body.

3 After tying in the tail, following Procedure 1, the fly is ready for completing the body.

QUILL GORDON
83

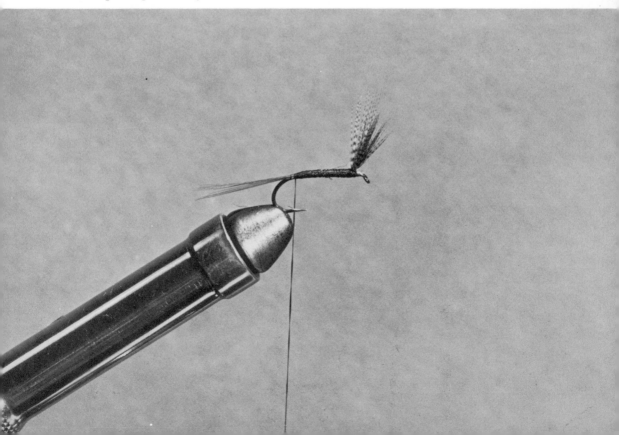

4 The body of this fly is made from the stripped quill from a peacock tail feather. Choose a feather which has the largest eye (the round figure, at the top of a male peacock tail feather, which has the appearance of an eye). Look at the reverse side of the eye. Examine the eye by using the thumb and forefinger to turn the quills sideways so the width may be inspected. Note that the quills in the lower part of the eye are wider as well as longer.

5 Cut the quill you have selected closely from the stalk.

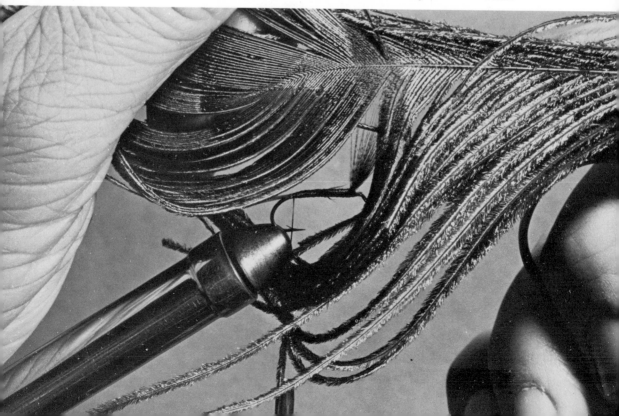

6 Lay the quill on a flat, light-colored surface, holding it in place with the left thumb 2 inches or more from the tip.

7 With a pencil eraser, rub along the quill, away from the thumb. This will remove the small fibers from one side of the quill after a few strokes.

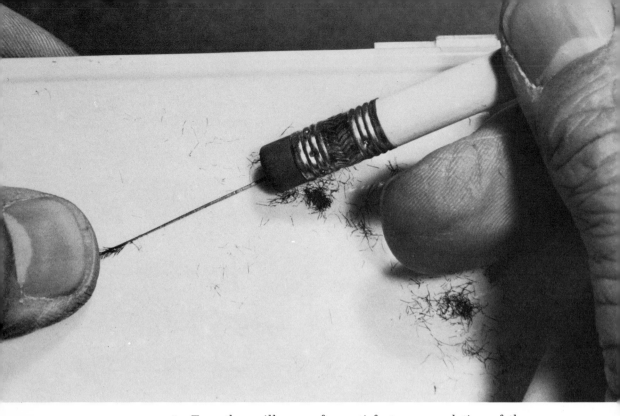

8 Turn the quill over after satisfactory completion of the previous step. Rub this side of the quill in the same manner with the eraser until it is completely stripped of the fibers, making it ready for use in the fly.

9 The quill is now ready for use. This is one of a number of methods of stripping a peacock quill.

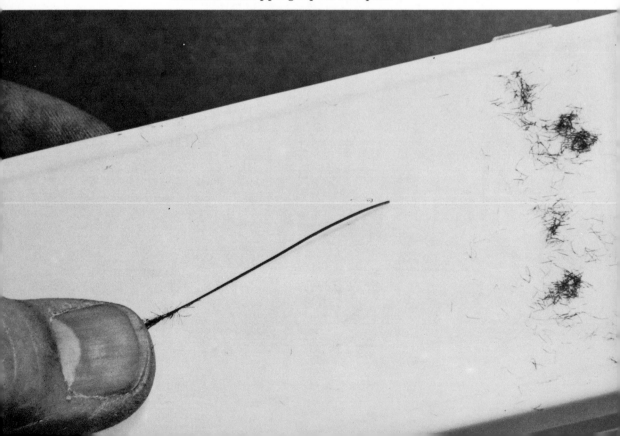

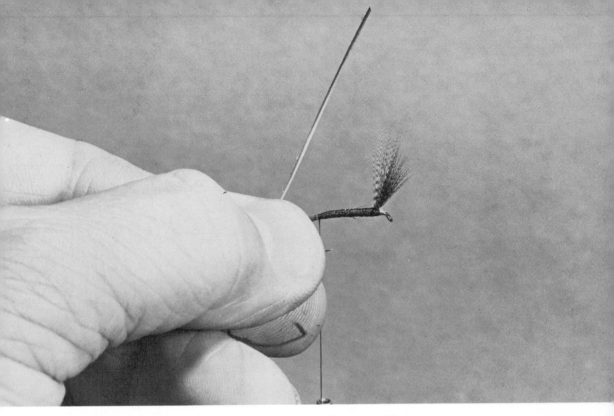

10 Examine the quill before tying it in. Note that one side has a dark stripe along the edge. When wrapped on, this will serve to create a ribbed appearance.

11 Tie in the quill beneath the hook at the rear of the body with the side showing the stripe on the underside, so that when wrapped, the stripe will show. Run thread to behind wings.

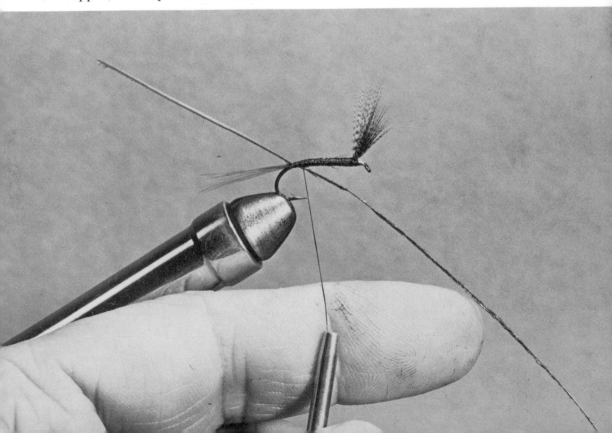

12 Wrap on the quill, using hackle pliers under light pressure, as peacock quill is extremely delicate. Continue these wraps to a point nearly three-quarters of the way to the eye of the hook and tie off.

13 Select two dark dun hackle feathers which have fibers as long as the hook shank. Remove the fibers from the lower third of the feathers.

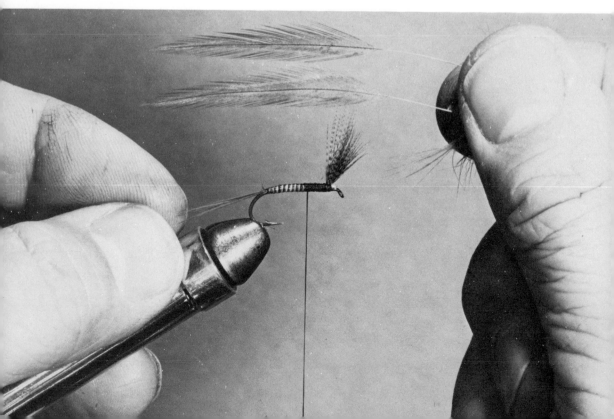

14 Tie in the dark dun hackles beneath the hook at the front of the body, with the good sides of the feathers facing the front of the fly.

15 After tying in securely, pull both hackles into upright position together as if you were beginning a wrap, and tie them into this position with their faces perpendicular to the hook shank and cut off stubs. Then run thread to behind hook eye.

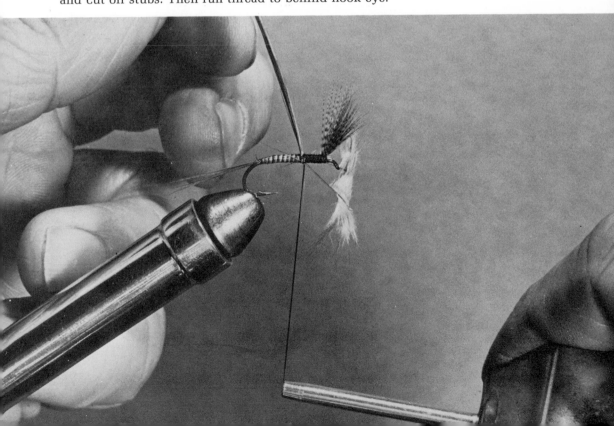

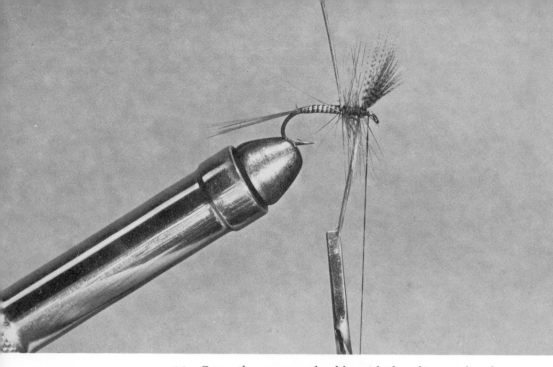

16 Grasp the rearmost hackle with the pliers and make one turn at the front of the body. The next turn should be angled forward so that the third turn will be right behind the wing. This will leave an obvious gap of thin hackle wrapping in the center. Make one more turn of the hackle behind the wing and another in front of the wing and tie off.

17 To tie off the hackle, complete the final turn of hackle, then use your left hand to make at least two turns of thread to tie down the hackle in place. Then you can take the thread in your right hand and make a few more turns for complete security. Hold the thread out of the way and cut the remainder of the feather off closely to the hook with the points of the scissors.

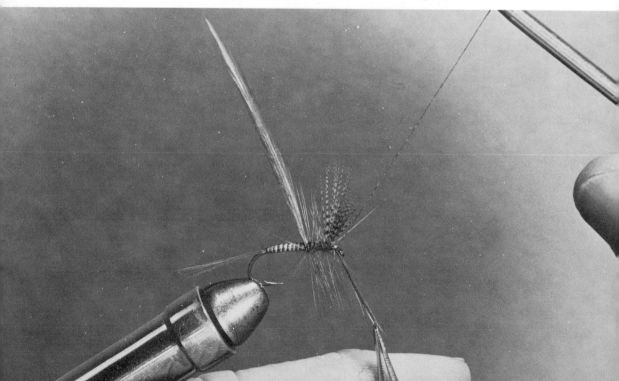

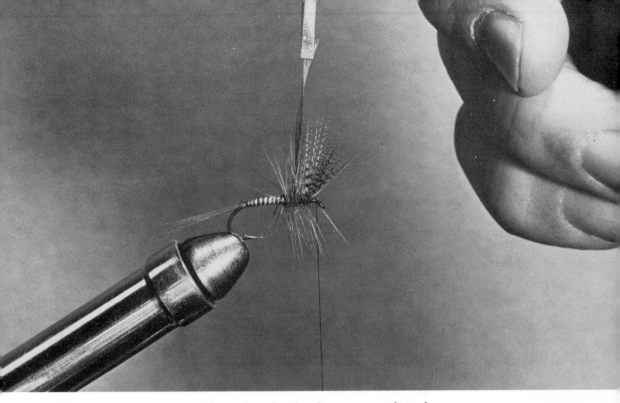

18 Grasp the other hackle and make the first turn angling forward to fill the gap which was left in wrapping the first hackle. Make two turns in this space and then another forward to make the final turn or two in front of the wings. During the wrapping of this second hackle, use a weaving motion to avoid binding down any of the hackle fibers.

19 Tie off the tip of the second hackle and the hackle is complete.

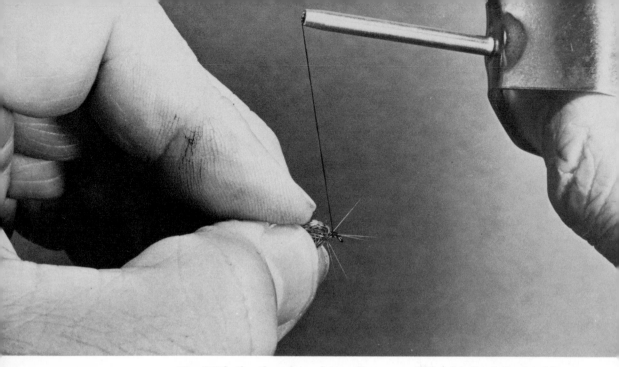

20 With the thumb and two fingers, pull back all of the hackle fibers and wing together to expose the head of the fly. This is to facilitate the wrapping of the tapered head, and will also reveal any small fibers that may have been caught up in the thread. They can be snipped off.

21 When the head is complete, release the fibers being held with the left hand and you will find that they all snap back into place. Complete whip finish and apply head cement. Final inspection of the fly may reveal some stray hackle fibers leaning back over the body of the fly, which may offend your sense of aesthetics. If so, these may be grasped firmly with the fingers and pulled forward to correct their position.

FEMALE BEAVERKILL

Materials used

Hook: #10 or #12 Model Perfect dry fly
Tail: brown hackle fibers
Body: gray muskrat underbody fur with
yellow chenille egg sac
Hackle: brown
Wing: mallard quill segments

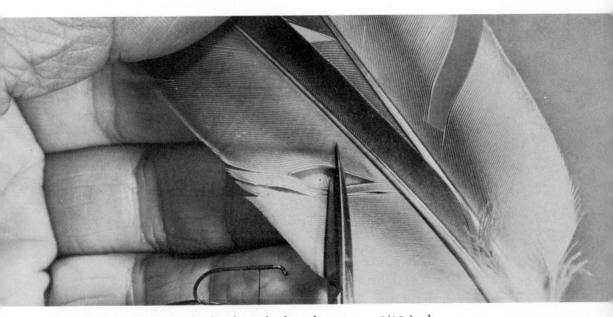

1 After covering hook shank with thread, cut one 3/16-inch-wide segment each from a left and a right mallard primary wing feather.

2 Preparatory to tying in, measure wing to be somewhat longer than the hook shank.

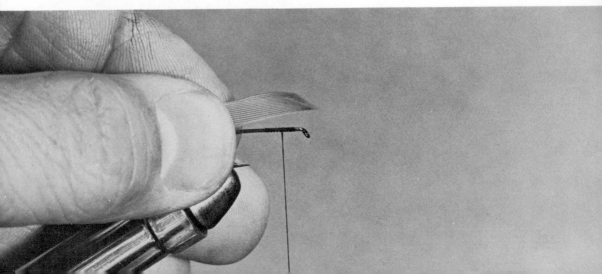

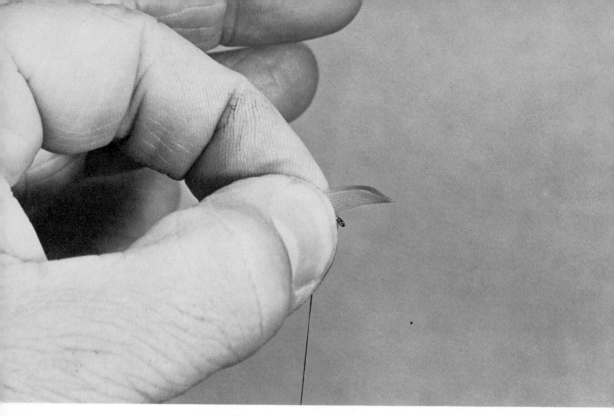

3 Using Procedure 2, pinch the wings together above the shank, making sure that the points of the quill segments are downward and forward.

4 Tie in the wings and then cut off the stubs.

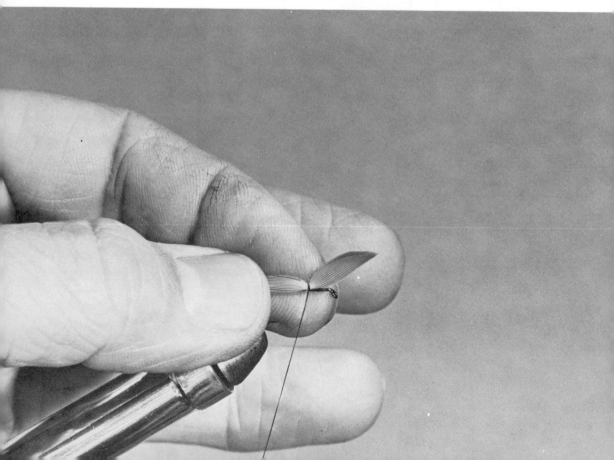

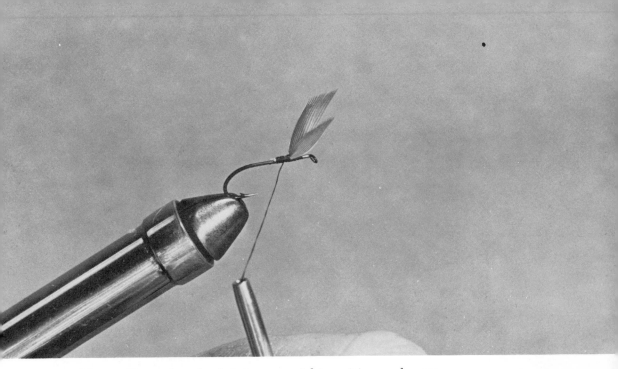

5 After pulling wings back into an upright position and wrapping a shoulder of thread in front to prop them into position, separate the wings (use your bodkin) and run thread in a figure-8 around the bases. During this operation the wings may be held in the desired upright position while placing the wraps of thread, to secure them in place.

6 Tie in the tail of brown hackle fibers. Select a 3-inch piece of fine yellow chenille, which is for the egg sac. Strip 3/8 inch of the thread core clean of the fuzzy fibers and tie in the thread core underneath the hook at bend.

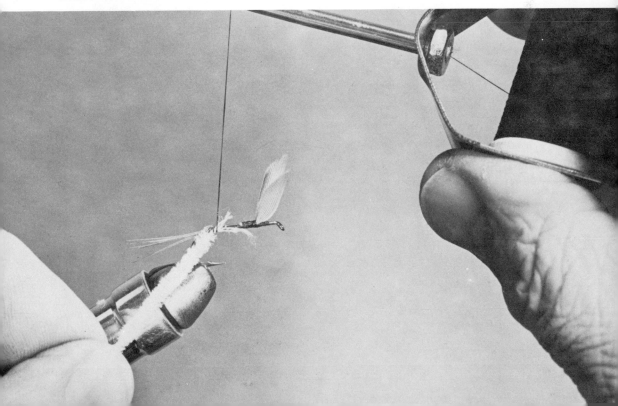

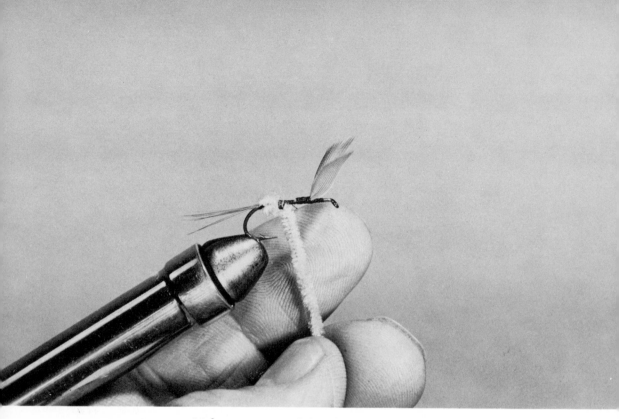

7 Make two turns of the chenille to create an egg sac about 1/8 inch long. Tie off chenille.

8 Put on a dubbed body of gray muskrat fur, leaving space behind wings for hackle.

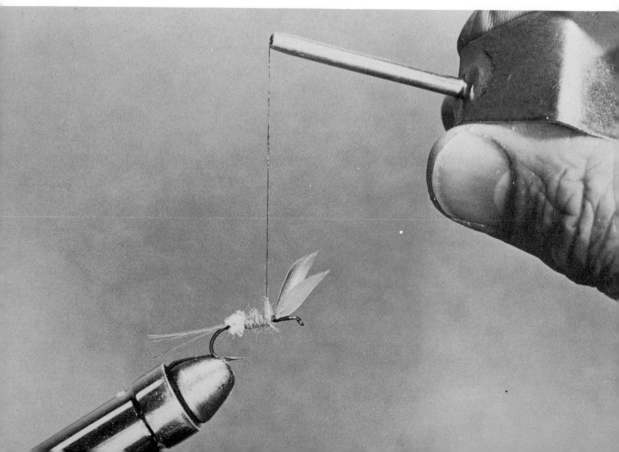

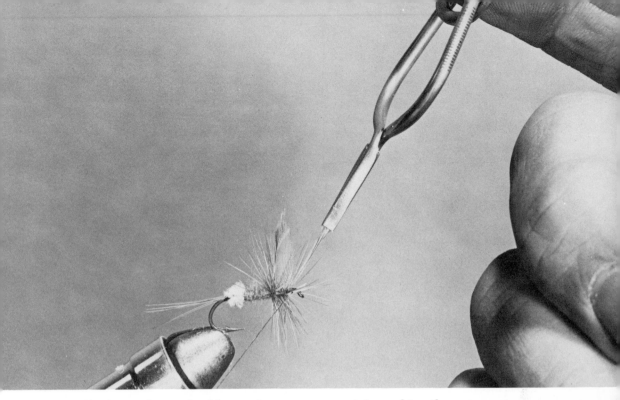

9 Tie in two brown hackles and wrap on separately, making the last two turns in front of the wings. During this operation, the wings sometimes get pushed forward to the wrong angle. If so, the final turns of hackle in front of the wings should be made while holding the wings back with the fingers.

10 Complete with whip finish and head cement.

IRRESISTIBLE

Materials used

Hook: #8 to #12 Model Perfect dry fly
Tail: brown deer body hair
Body: clipped deer body hair
Hackle: dark dun
Wing: brown bucktail

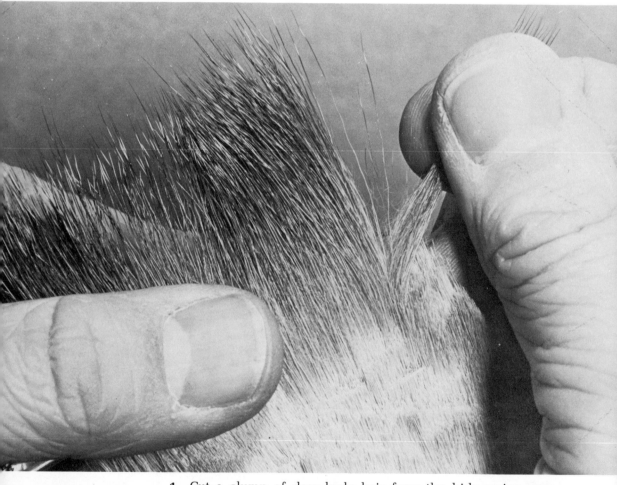

1 Cut a clump of deer body hair from the hide, using your heavier scissors. Remove underbody fur from the base of the hairs.

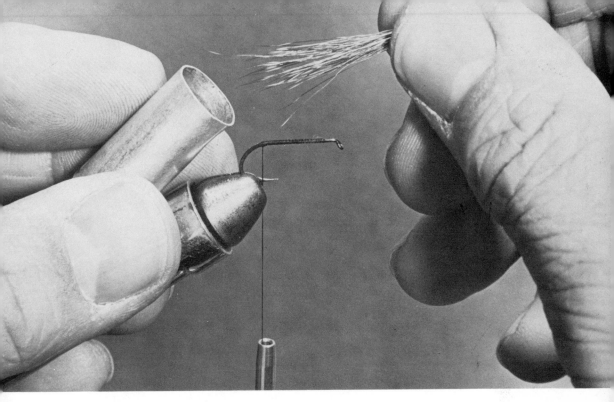

2 Insert the hairs, tips first, into a small cylindrical tube, such as a lipstick cover.

3 Tap the butts of the hairs lightly with the finger, and also tap the tube bottom on the tabletop, to even the ends.

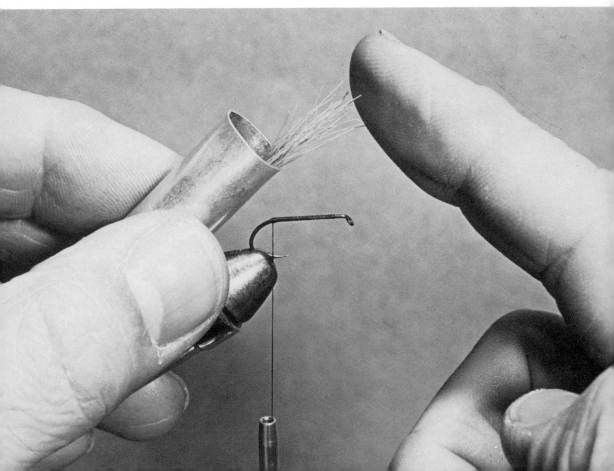

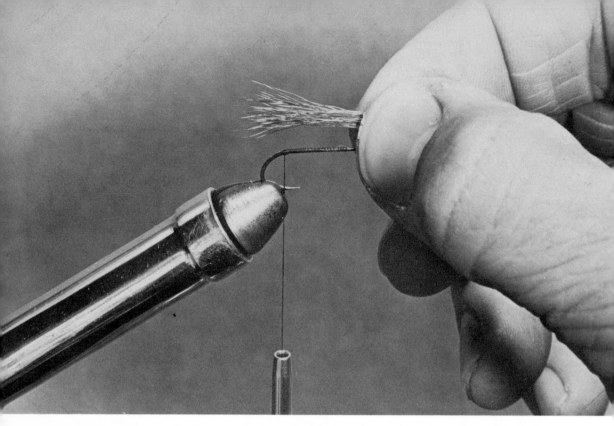

4 Remove hairs, pinching to keep tips aligned, and measure along hook shank so that when tied in for the tail, they will be as long as the shank of the hook.

5 Hold the hair clump at an angle to the hook, just over the beginning of the bend, and make one light turn of thread while at this angle.

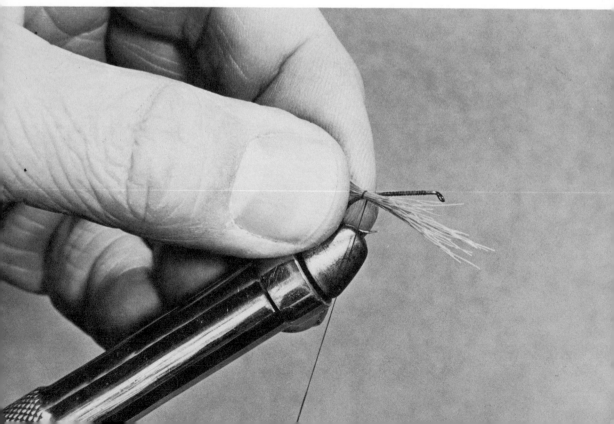

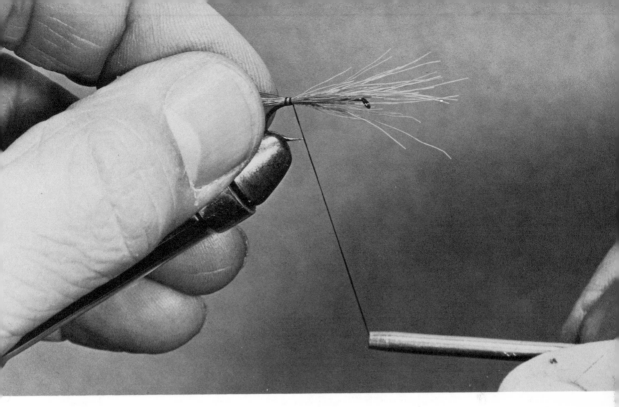

6 Make a second turn, but at the same time, bring the tail into position straight along the hook shank. Make two more turns and release the left hand, as the tail should now be held in proper position by the thread. Then make a few more turns forward, cut off the stubs remaining, and make more turns to cover the stubs smoothly.

7 Cut another clump of deer body hair, larger than the first one.

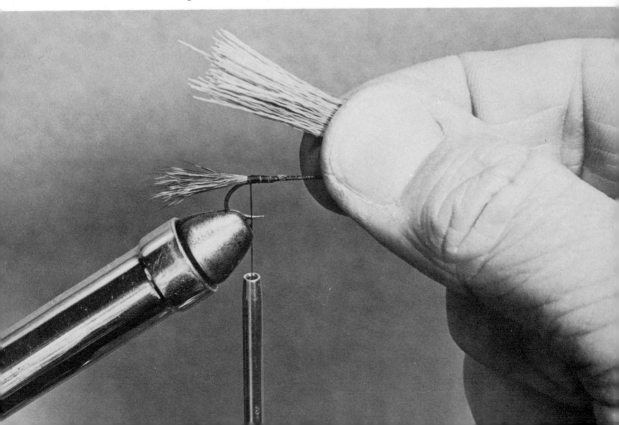

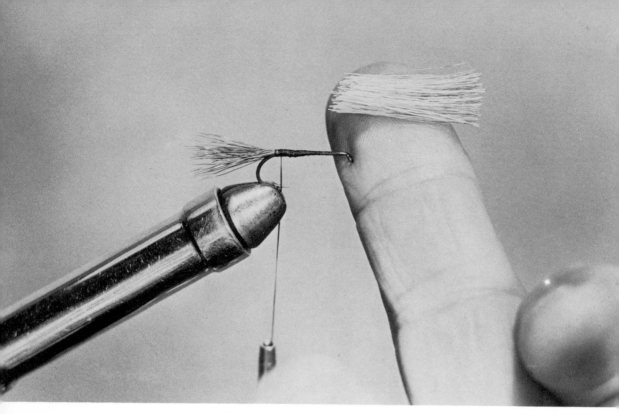

8 Cut off tip ends.

9 Angle hairs away and to the right and bring one turn of thread lightly over at a point just ahead of where the tail is tied in. Make a second turn of thread, and on the downward movement with the thread, release the hairs from the fingers and pull rather tightly.

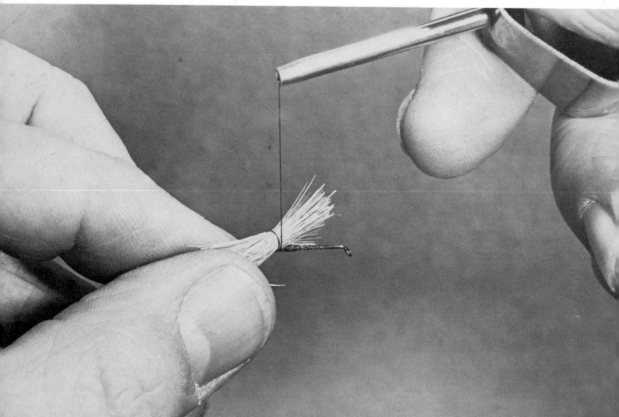

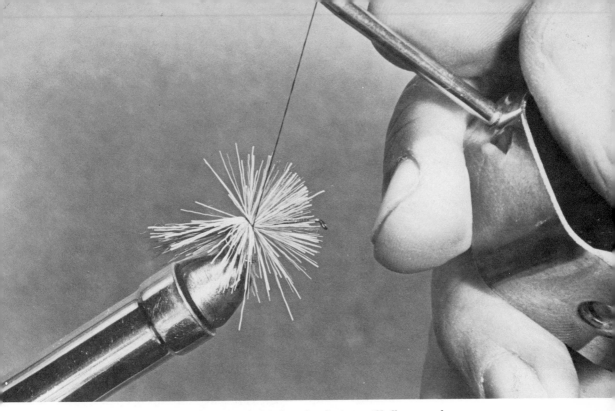

10 If you have done step 9 properly, the hairs will flare and move around the hook shank as shown. Some hairs may catch on hook point. If so, free them with the dubbing needle.

11 Make a second turn and immediately pull all of the hairs back with the left hand to expose the hook shank. Wrap thread in front of this hair.

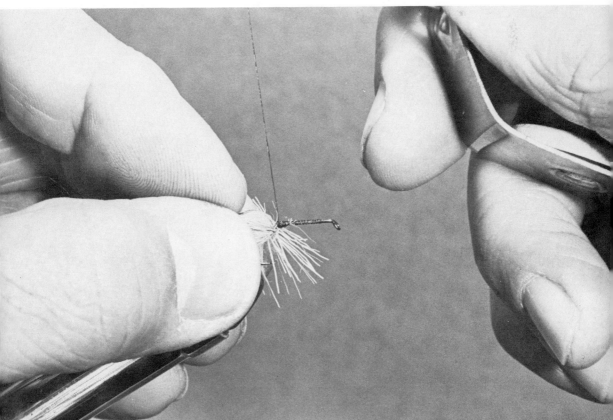

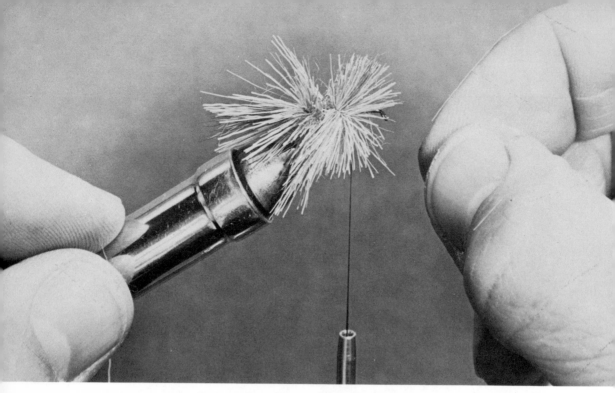

12 Cut another clump of deer body hairs and repeat steps 8–11, tying in more hair in front of the first body clump.

13 After this clump is tied in, push the whole mass toward the rear of the hook with the fingers of the right hand. Tie in still another clump of hairs and push them back on the hook too.

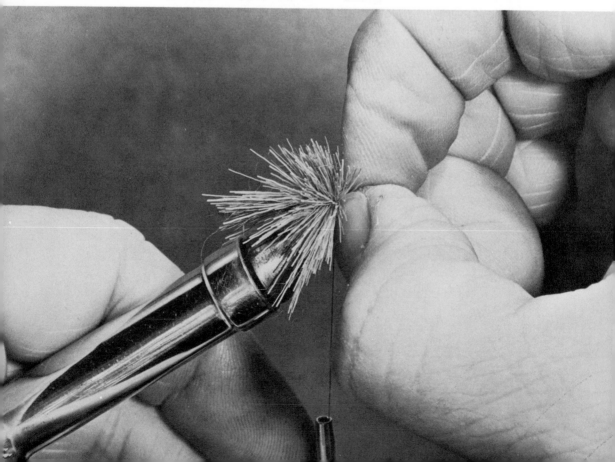

14 After all of the hair is tied on, make many wraps in front to hold it in place.

15 Use the scissor points to form the body, holding them parallel to the shank.

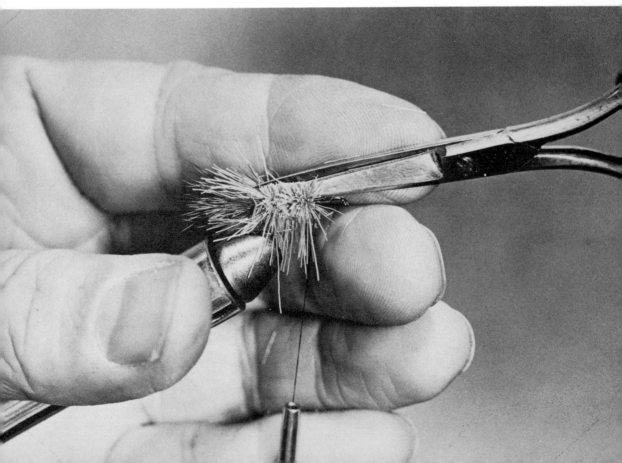

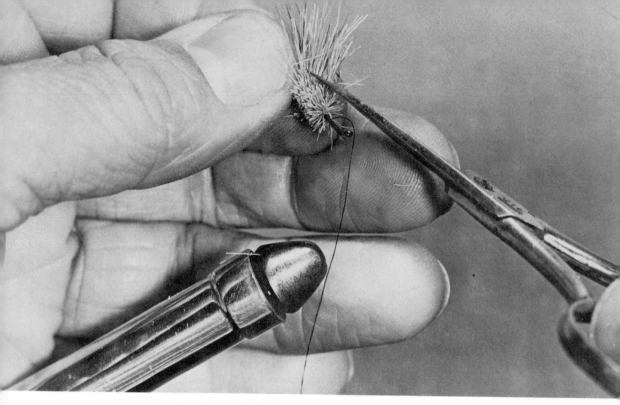

16 You will find it necessary to complete the clipping opera-tion with the fly held in either your fingers or the hackle pliers.

17 When the body has been completely clipped, with a slight taper as shown, replace the fly in the vise.

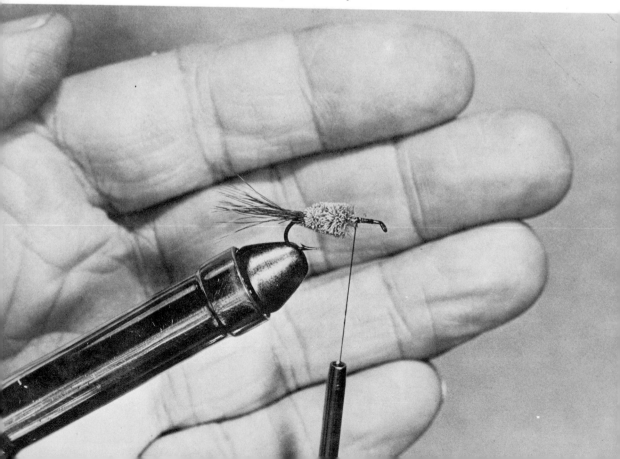

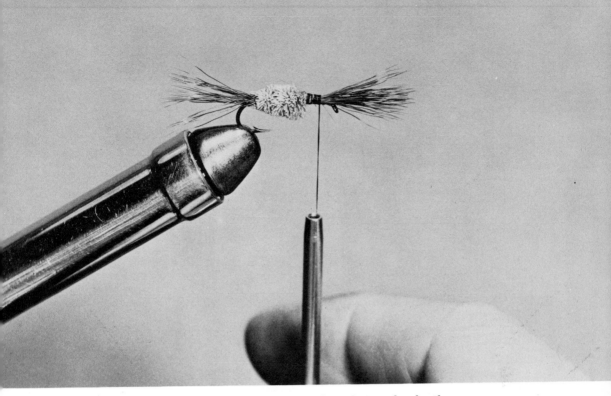

18 Remove a small clump of dark-brown hair from a bucktail, even up the tips as in steps 2–3, and tie in, just ahead of the body, for wings.

19 Complete the wings, separating them and holding them in position with figure-8 winds (Procedure 2).

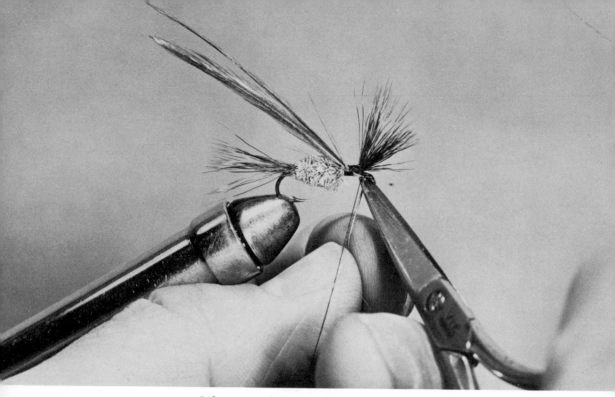

20 Select two dark dun hackle feathers and tie them in. Then wrap each separately, as described in the instructions for tying the Quill Gordon dry fly.

21 Complete the whip finish and apply head cement to the finished fly.

ADAMS SPENTWING

Materials used

> Hook: #12 to #16 Model Perfect dry fly
> Tail: mixed brown and grizzly hackle fibers
> Body: gray muskrat underbody fur
> Hackle: mixed brown and grizzly hackle, one each
> Wing: grizzly hackle tips

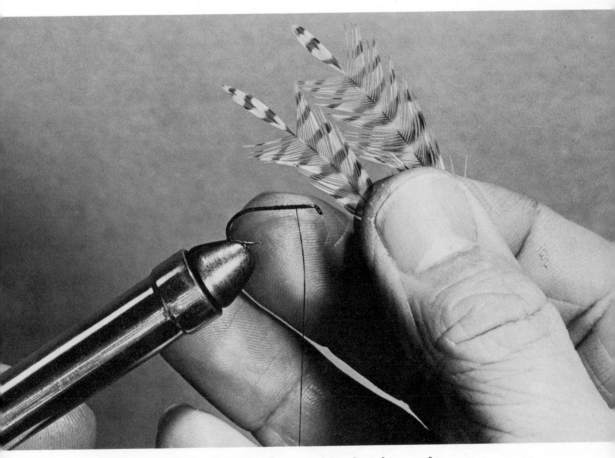

1 After fastening the thread on the hook and making a few turns of thread for a base on which to put the wing, select two grizzly hackles of uniform tip shape and pull back the hackle fibers to leave enough of the tip to be wings.

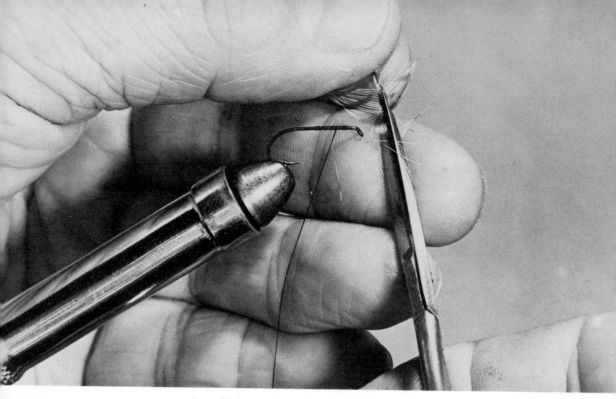

2 Cut off the pulled-back hackle fibers fairly close to the stem of the hackles, leaving short stubs which will aid in keeping the wings in proper position on the hook. Hackle tip wings have a tendency to twist when tied in, making the wing angle incorrect.

3 The prepared wings before tying in.

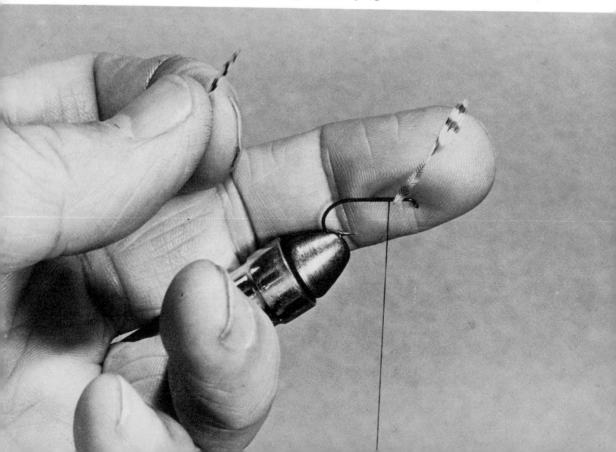

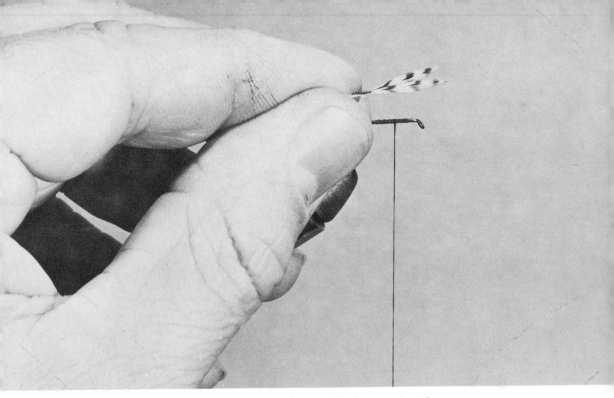

4 Place the two hackle points together with the good sides facing each other.

5 Tie the wings on, following Procedure 2. Then grasp them, pull them back beyond the upright position, make numerous turns of thread close in front as a shoulder to prop them in an upright position.

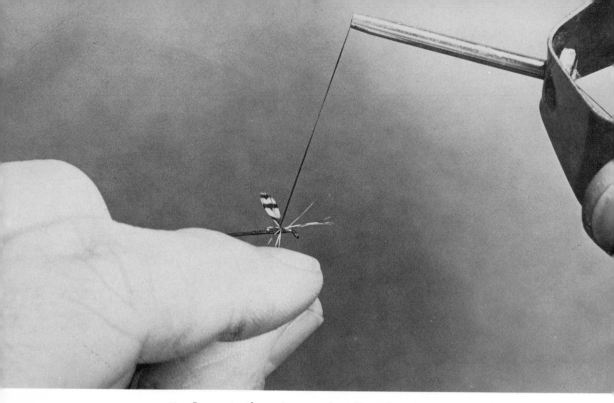

6 Separate the wings and pull each wing out to a horizontal position and run the thread in a figure-8 around the bases, holding one wing at a time in the horizontal position and wrapping the thread so that each is secured into that position.

7 Tie in a tail of mixed brown and grizzly hackle fibers.

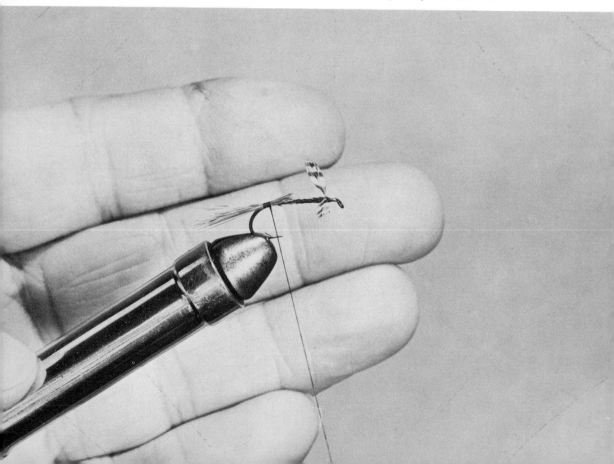

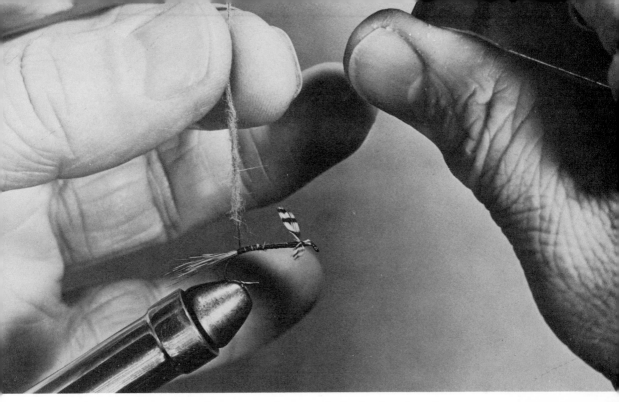

8 Prepare a "rope" of gray muskrat underbody fur for the dubbed body.

9 Wind dubbing forward nearly two-thirds of the way to the eye and tie off, leaving space for the hackle.

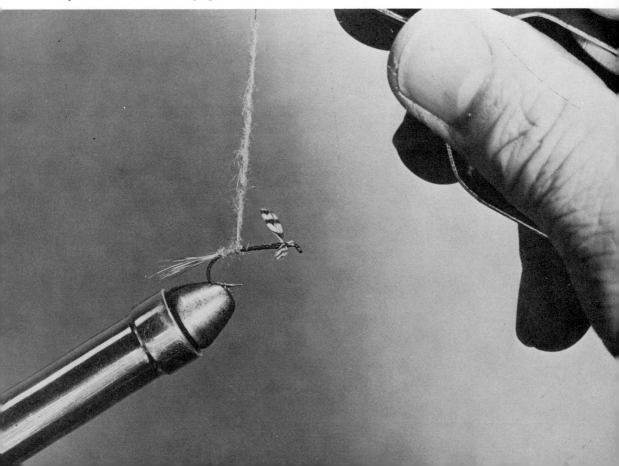

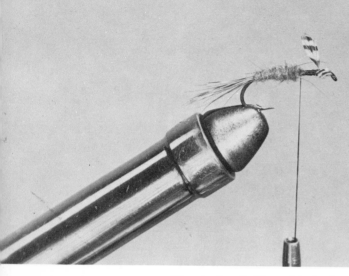

10   As in all flies, this body too must be tapered.

11   Choose one grizzly and one brown hackle and strip off fibers at the base, removing the greatest part of the web, as well as fibers too long for this fly.

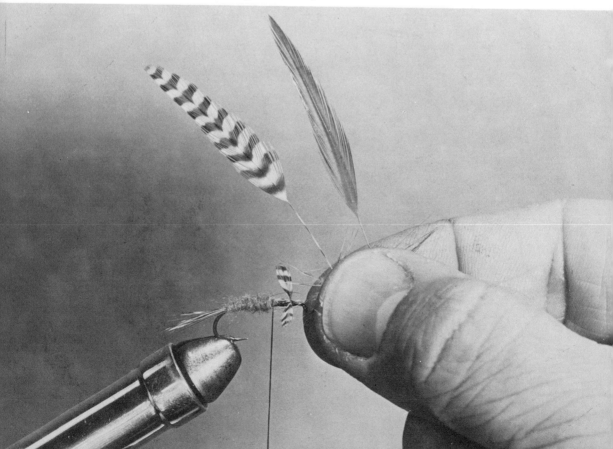

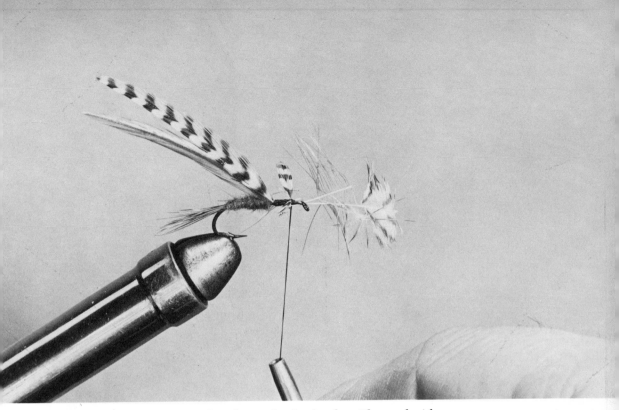

12 Tie in hackles together beneath the hook with good sides facing forward.

13 Grasp hackles separately with the hackle pliers and wrap on separately, as described for the Quill Gordon.

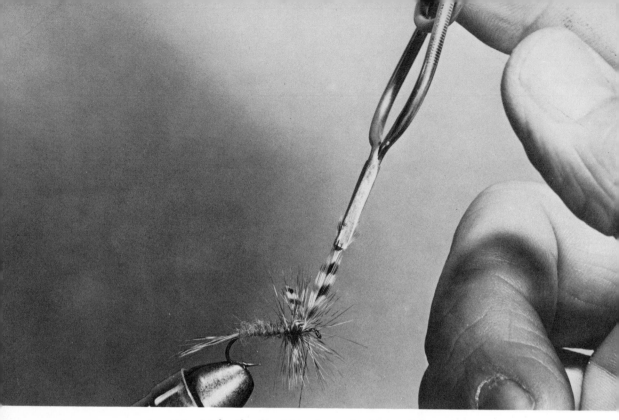

14 Make the final two turns in front of the wings.

15 Wrap tapered head, complete whip finish, and apply head cement.

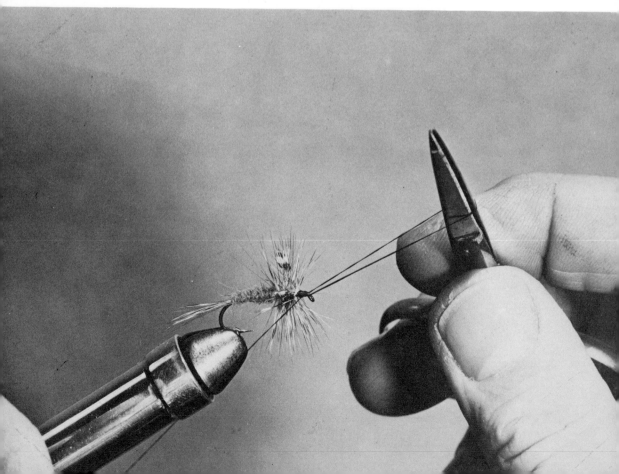

CADDIS FLY

Materials used

Hook: #12 to #22 Model Perfect dry fly
Tail: none
Body: gray muskrat fur
Hackle: brown
Wing: brown deer hair, down-wing

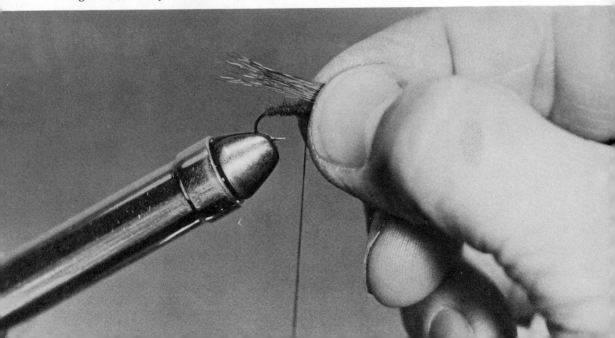

1 This fly will have no tail, so after applying the base of thread, immediately wrap on a dubbed body of gray fur, to a point about three-quarters of the way to the eye of the hook.

2 Cut some deer body hairs from the skin and remove the underbody hairs from the base of the clump. Measure along the hook to determine where they must be tied in to have half their length extend beyond the body. Make sure tips are even.

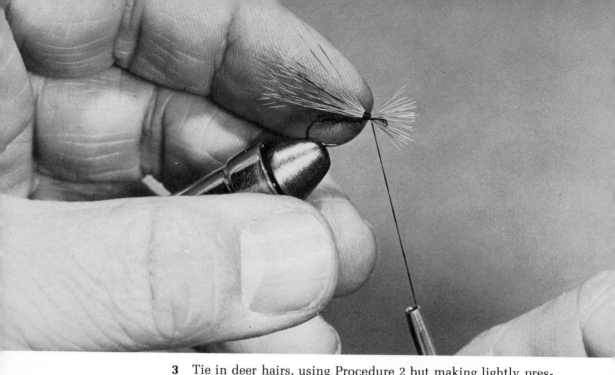

3 Tie in deer hairs, using Procedure 2 but making lightly pressured wraps of the thread at first. This will control, somewhat, the flaring of the deer hair, caused by its hollowness. Flaring can be controlled further, if necessary, by applying a drop of head cement just behind the thread wraps and allowing it to dry while holding the hairs together with the fingers.

4 When satisfied with this step, wrap the thread forward, cut off the hair stubs and cover them completely with thread. Make sure the covering of thread is smooth, as the hackle must be wrapped over this.

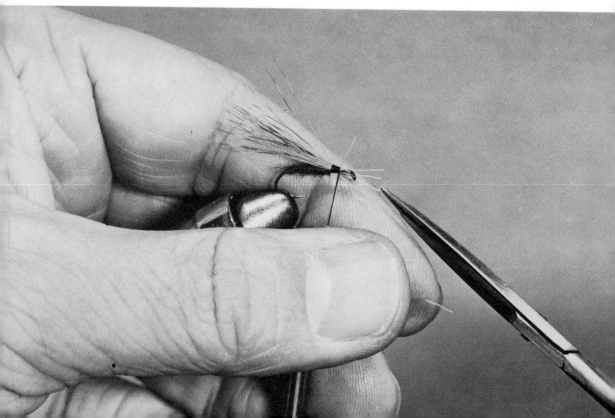

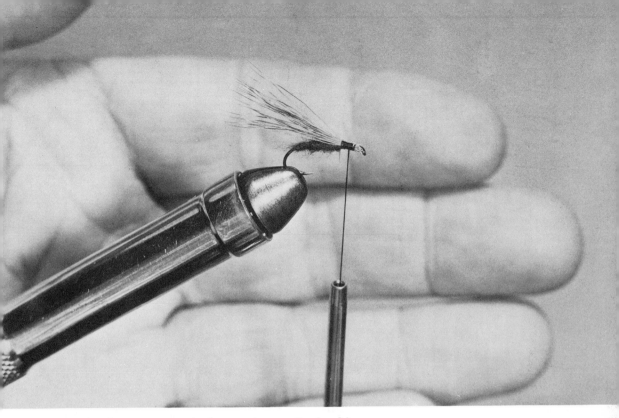

5 The fly is now ready for putting on the hackle.

6 Tie in one brown hackle feather of appropriate size for this fly, and wrap forward closely for three or four turns and tie off.

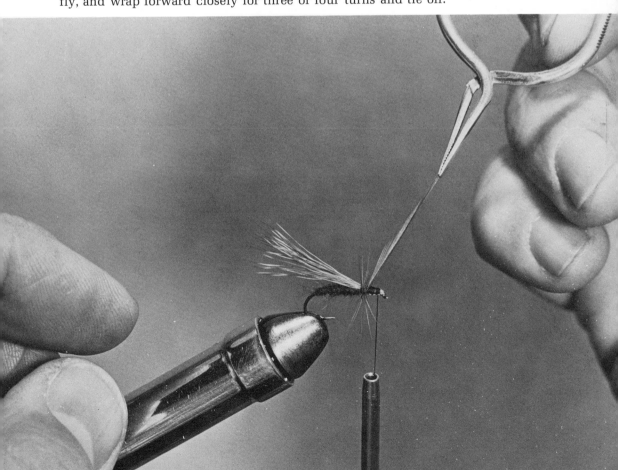

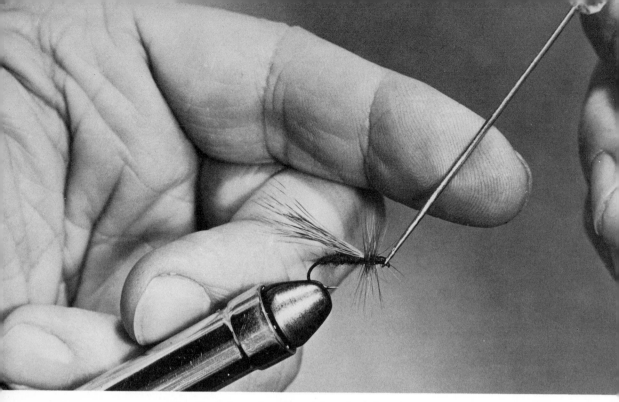

7 Complete the fly with whip finish and apply head cement.

8 You may wish to clip off the bottom hackle fibers. This practice is becoming increasingly popular with innovative fishermen and fly-tiers. If so, remove the fly from the vise, turn it upside down, and clip closely, leaving lateral hackle fibers untouched.

SPIDER

Materials used

Hook: #12 to #16 dry fly, turned-up eye
Tail: none
Body: medium gold tinsel
Hackle: brown saddle hackle, large
Wing: none

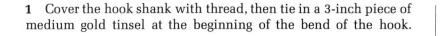

1   Cover the hook shank with thread, then tie in a 3-inch piece of medium gold tinsel at the beginning of the bend of the hook.

2   After running thread forward, wrap the tinsel toward the eye to a point just forward of the center of the hook.

SPIDER
121

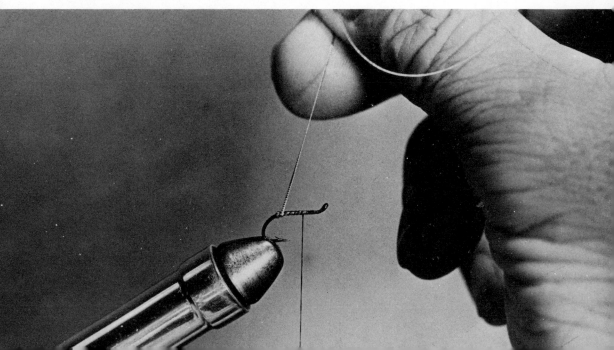

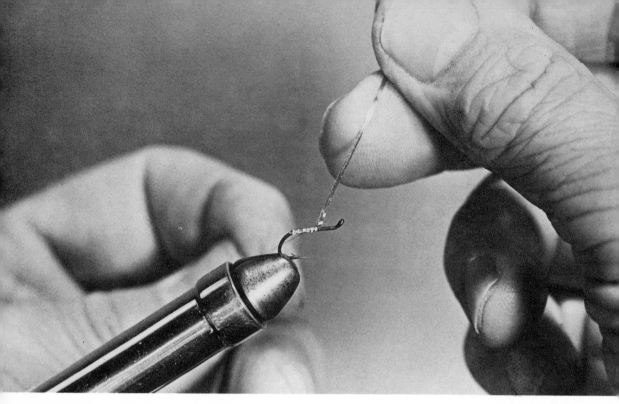

3 Tie off and cut off excess tinsel.

4 Select one brown saddle hackle of best quality available with longest, stiffest fibers. Remove webbed fibers and tie in, in front of the gold body. Hackles with a fiber length of over an inch are not too long for making Spiders.

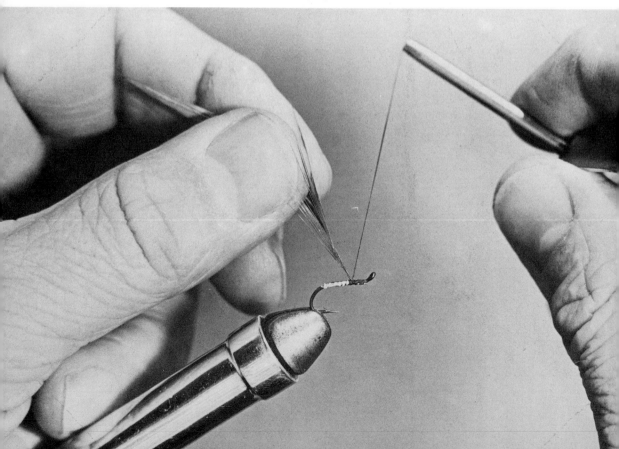

5 Wrap forward four turns, close together. Tie off and cut off excess hackle.

6 The hooks with turned-up eyes present a little more problem in making the head. However, as in most other dry flies, pull all of the hackles back together with the fingers and, leaving the head exposed, wrap many turns of thread to shape the head. Then release the hackle fibers and complete the whip finish.

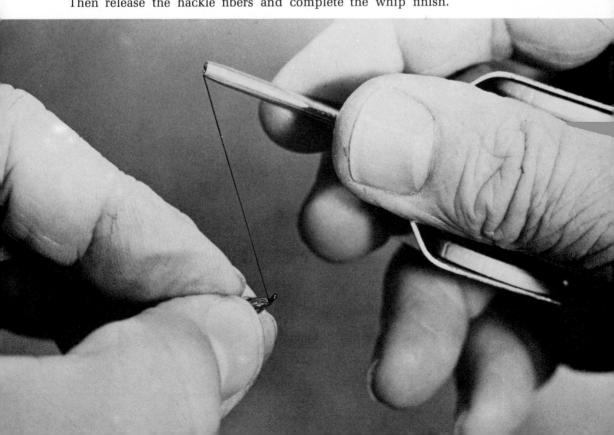

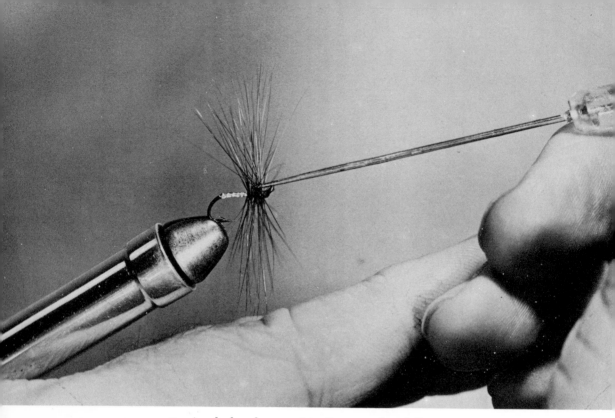

7 Apply head cement to the completed fly.

8 Generally, if some of the hackle fibers appear displaced, they can be pulled into position with the fingers so that the fly will have the classic silhouette.

8
Nymphs

A NYMPH IS THE LARVAL FORM OF AN AQUATIC INSECT. MOST OF
a trout's diet consists of insects that live in the water as nymphs,
then rise to the surface, shuck their larval covering, and emerge
as adult winged flies. The mayfly—which in most streams is by
far the most important insect to the trout—is an example. The
nymph, of course, looks completely different from the adult,
just as a caterpillar seems to bear no relation to a moth.

Some nymph imitations are tied to represent particular
species of insects. The three patterns explained in this chapter,
however, are more general patterns and can be used to represent
a wide range of larvae. The last nymph, an emerger, has wings,
since it represents the moment of transition from nymph to
adult.

FLOSS BODY—CONVENTIONAL

Materials used

> Hook: #10 to #14 1X Model Perfect wet fly
> Tail: brown hackle fibers
> Body: yellow floss with rib of black thread
> Wing case: cinnamon turkey tail feather segment
> Abdomen: peacock herl
> Legs: brown hackle

1 Cover hook shank with thread and put on tail of brown
hackle fibers, fully as long as the overall hook shank. Tie in a
4-inch piece of black tying thread and leave hanging.

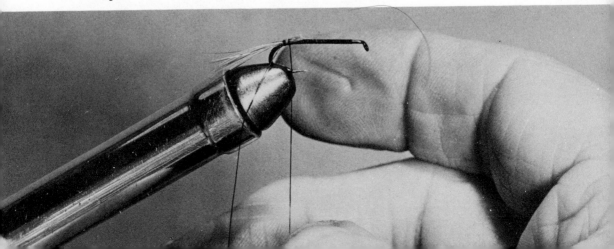

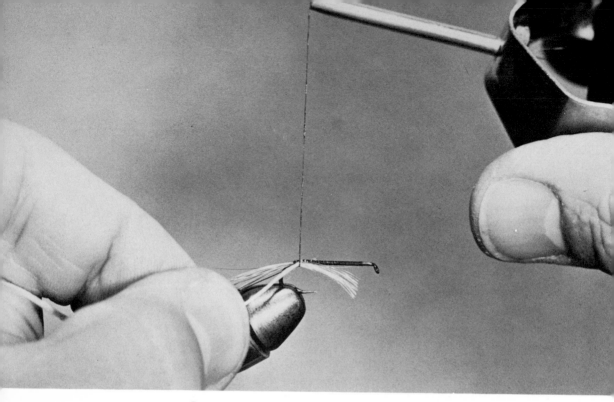

2 Cut a piece of yellow silk floss 8 inches long and tie it in at the bend of the hook.

3 Wind on a body, making it heavier in the front portion to create the tapered appearance. The body should run fully three-quarters of the way to the eye of the hook.

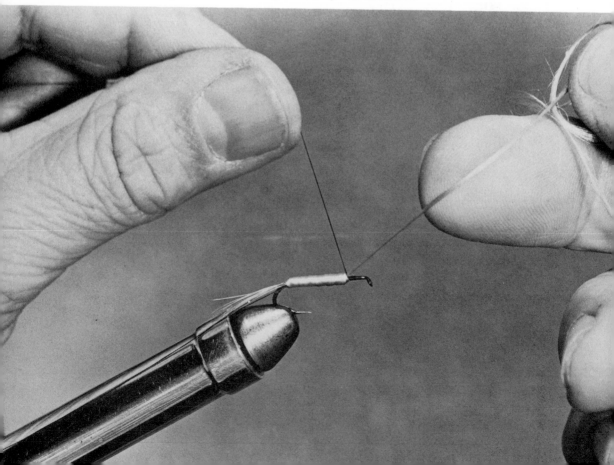

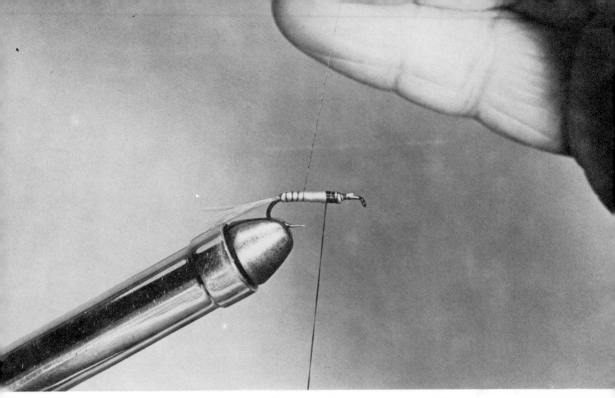

4 Wind on the black thread with even spaces to create a rib.

5 Tie off the black thread with the tying thread at the front of the body.

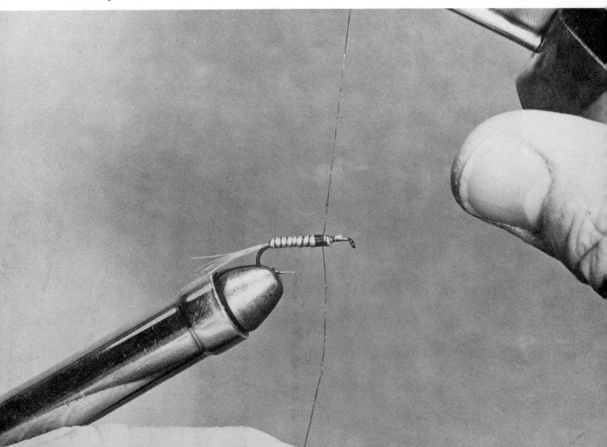

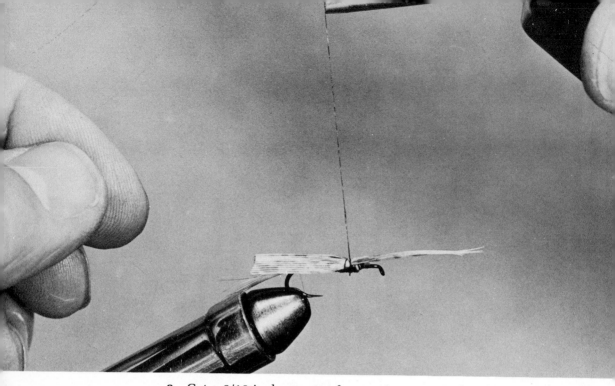

6 Cut a 3/16-inch segment from a cinnamon turkey feather. Invert segment and tie in by the tip at the front part of the body. Since this segment must lie flat after being tied in, use light turns of thread in the first wraps, to avoid separating the fibers, and tie it in firmly in later wraps forward of the first turns.

7 Prepare a brown hackle by removing about a third of the lower fibers on the feather. The size of this hackle can be determined in the same manner as for a dry fly, with a little generosity on the fiber length. Tie in but don't wind on the hackle yet.

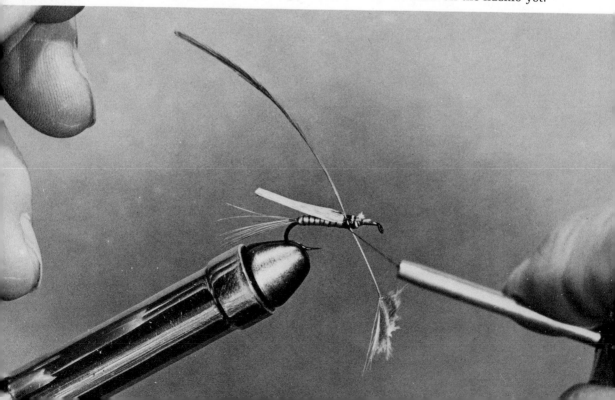

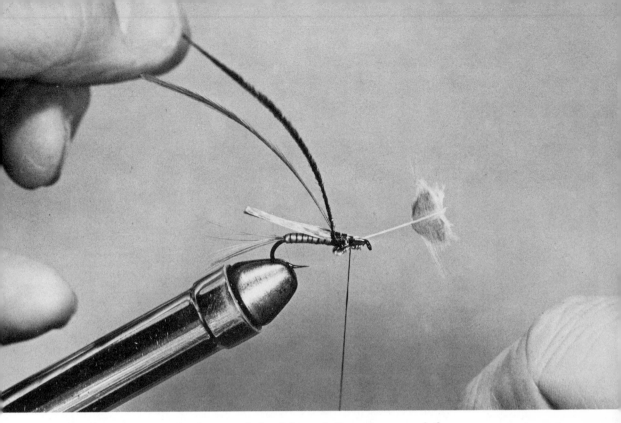

8   Choose a strand of peacock herl from below the eye of the feather and tie it in about 2 inches from the tip end. Cut off all stubs. Run thread to behind eye.

9   Wrap the peacock herl forward, leaving space for the head.

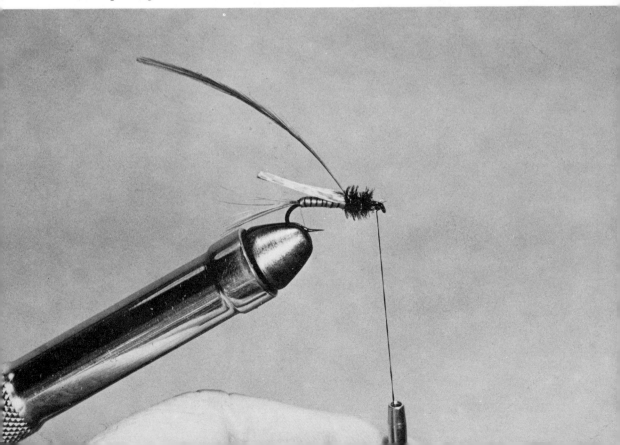

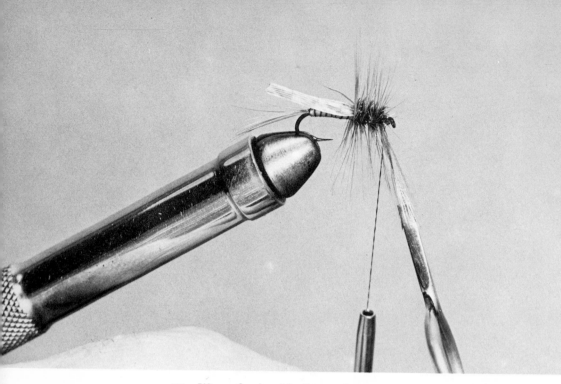

10 Wrap the hackle forward, using a weaving action to avoid binding down the peacock herl and again leaving space for the head.

11 After tying off the hackle, trim all of the fibers off the top of the fly, to prepare way for the wing case to be drawn forward. This should leave only the fibers protruding laterally and below.

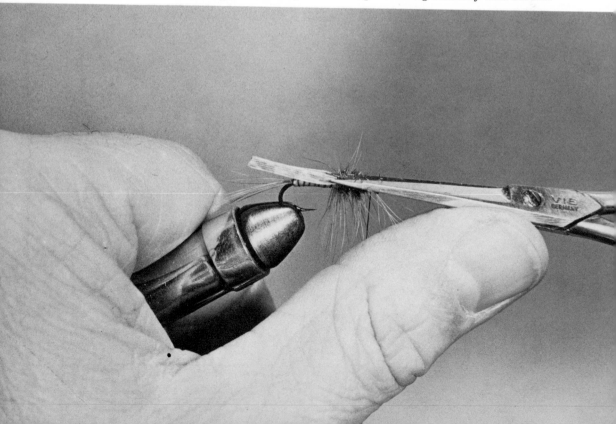

12 Grasp the wing-case segment, pull it forward with the right hand, and bring the tying thread up over lightly with the left hand to bind down the quill at the head. Hold this quill taut while tying down, so that a triangular wing case will result.

13 After the two first turns, three or four more turns may be made tightly to secure the wing case. Cut off the remaining stub of the wing case and the head can be completed.

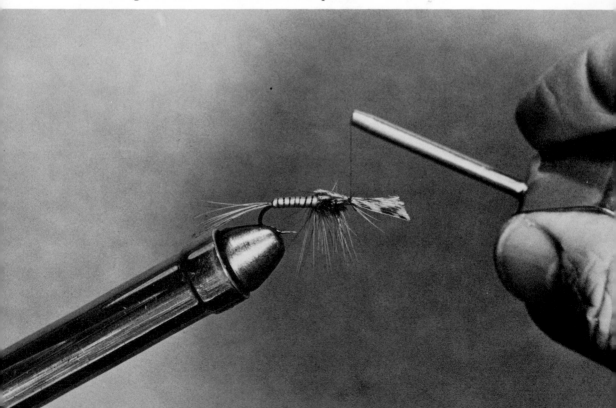

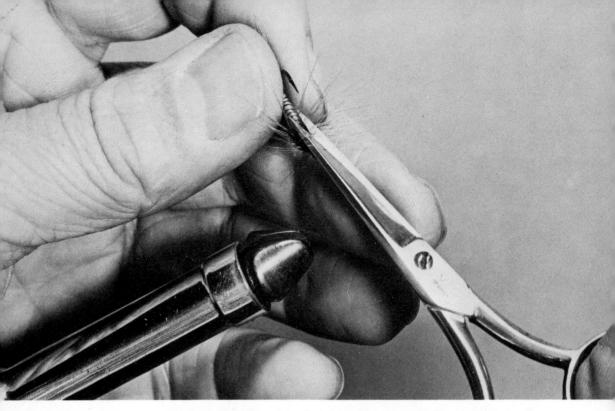

14 Complete the whip finish and cement the head. Remove fly from vise and turn over to expose the underside. Clip off the underside hackle fibers with the scissors, leaving short stubs by not clipping too close.

15 The finished nymph should now have legs to the sides only.

HARE'S EAR

Materials used

    Hook: #10 to #16 2X Model Perfect wet fly
    Tail: brown partridge fibers
    Body: hare's-ear fur with gold rib
    Wing case: dark turkey quill segment
    Thorax: hare's-ear fur
    Legs: brown partridge

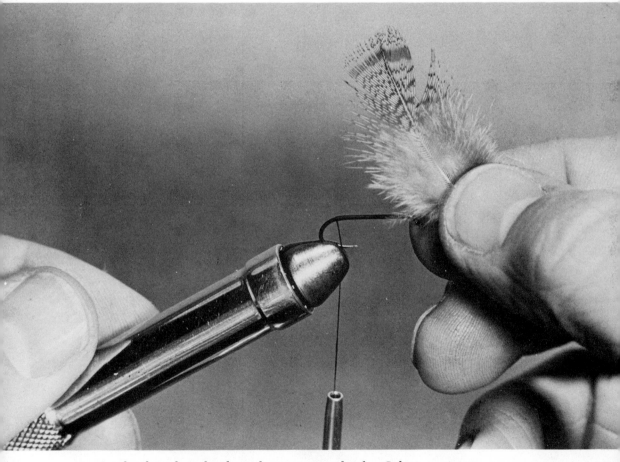

1 Apply thread to hook and cover completely. Select a partridge feather of medium-brown shade, fibers of which will be used for the tail of this nymph.

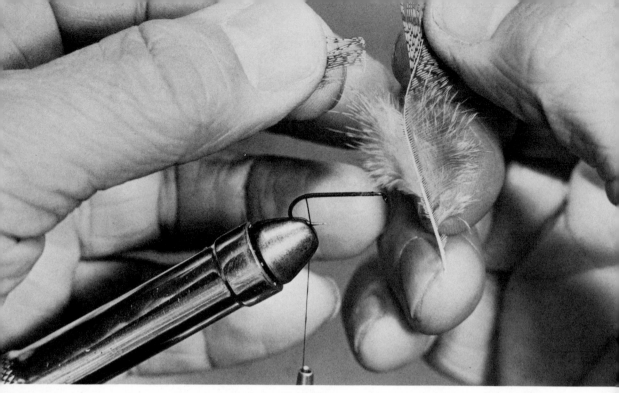

2 Tear some of the fibers from the stem, selecting those which are straight. Tie in as a tail.

3 Preparatory to making a dubbed body of hare's-ear fur, rub some fly-tying wax on the thread. Hare's-ear fur (selected from the base of the ears) is one of the more difficult dubbing materials, because it is relatively coarse. The wax makes a sticky base for the fur to adhere to. Apply the fur to the thread, but do not wrap it yet.

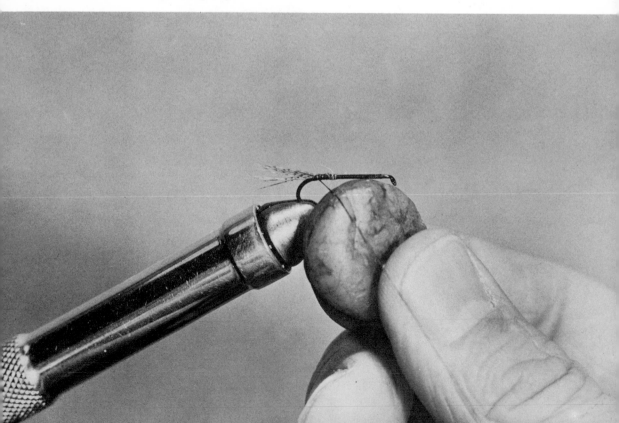

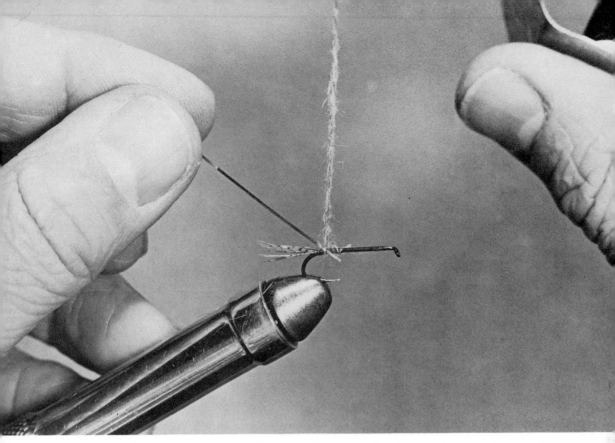

4   Tie in a piece of medium gold tinsel about 4 inches long to be the rib.

5   Wrap on the dubbed body, leaving the tinsel hanging for the next step.

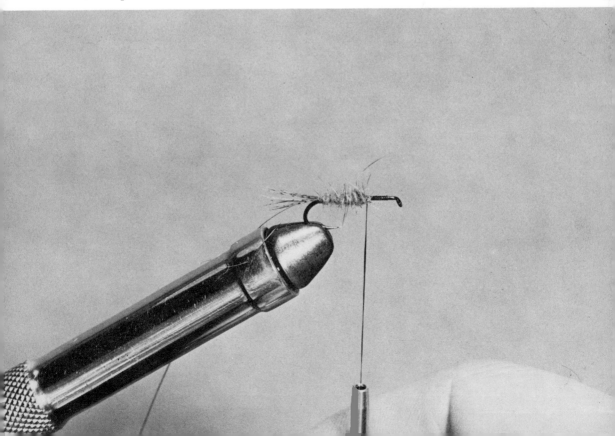

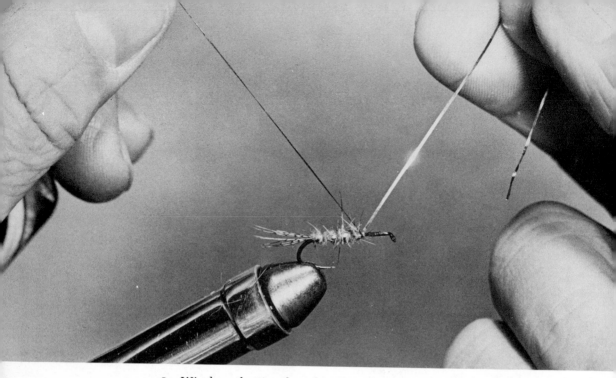

6 Wind on the tinsel, making evenly separated wraps as shown, and tie off.

7 Cut a 3/16-inch-wide segment out of a dark-brown turkey feather. Sometimes it is difficult to remove exactly the width of segment desired. If so, cut a larger segment than you want and then remove the excess fibers with the point of the dubbing needle.

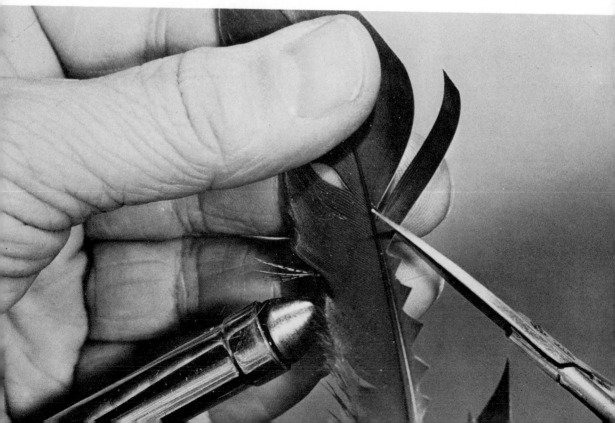

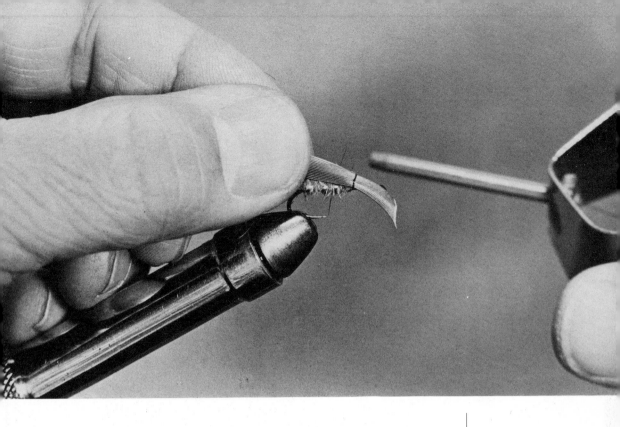

8 & 9 Tie in the tip of the quill segment on top of the shank, with the good side down (it will be folded over later).

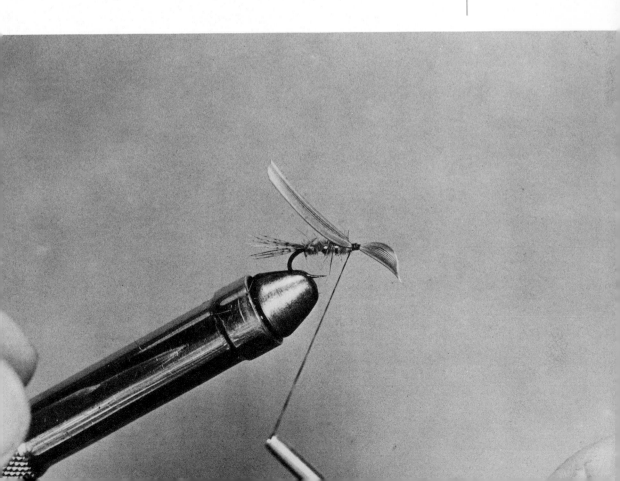

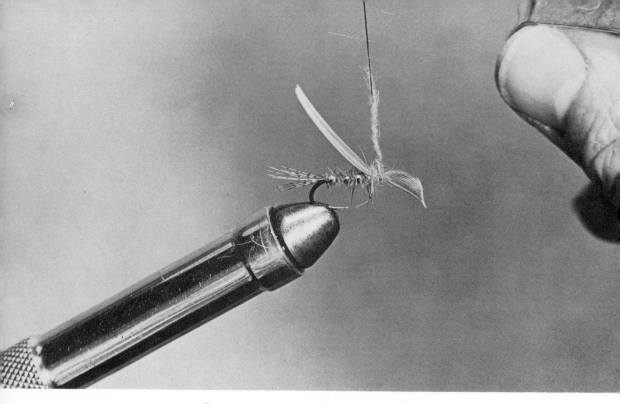

10   Prepare some more hare's-ear dubbing to be wrapped on for the thorax. When winding on, create an obvious lump to approximate the anatomy of a natural nymph. Run thread back to rear of thorax.

11   Choose a small brown partridge feather and stroke back all of the fibers except for a few on the tip of the feather. Since only the six or so fibers nearest the top of the pulled-back ones will be used for the legs, a number of the lower ones may be removed from the stem.

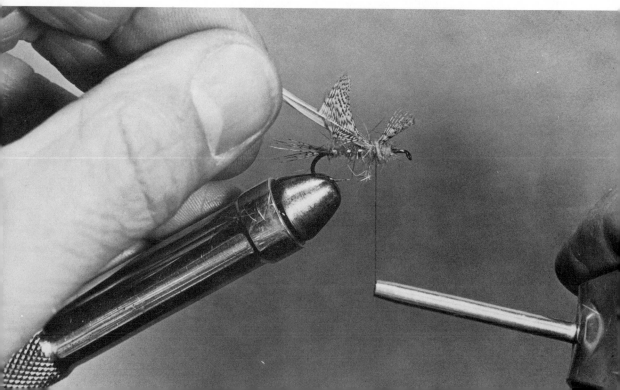

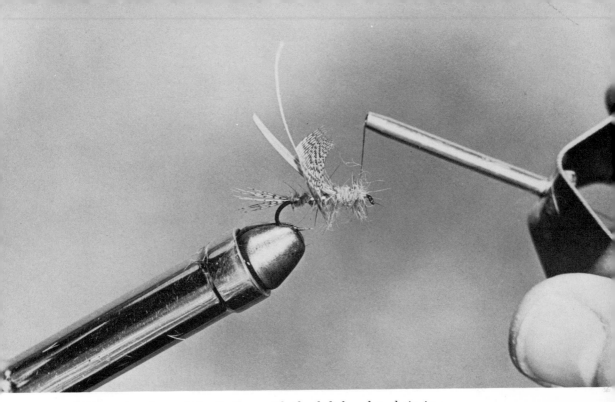

12 Grasp the stem of the feather with the left hand and tie in the exposed tip while holding the feather upside down, with the tip pointing to the right lying over the thorax. The point of tie-in is where the wing-case feather exits from beneath the rear of the thorax. Return the thread to behind the hook eye.

13 Grasp the stem of the partridge feather and pull it up over the eye of the hook. Tie down securely and cut off remainder.

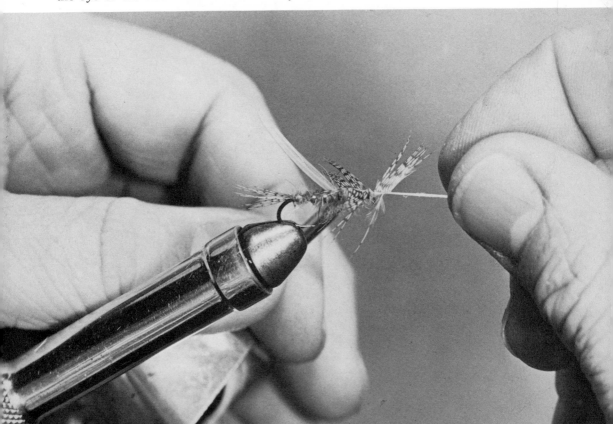

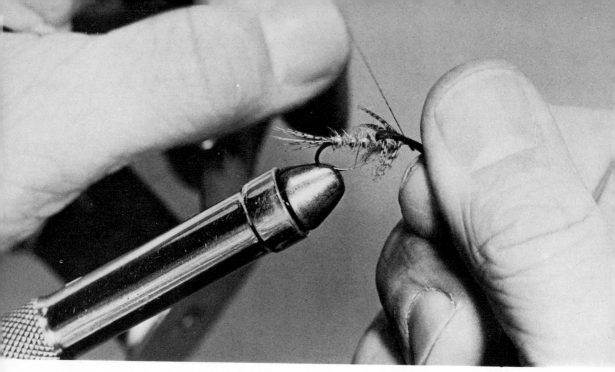

14 Pull the wing-case feather forward and tie down.

15 Make a few more wraps and cut off the stub.

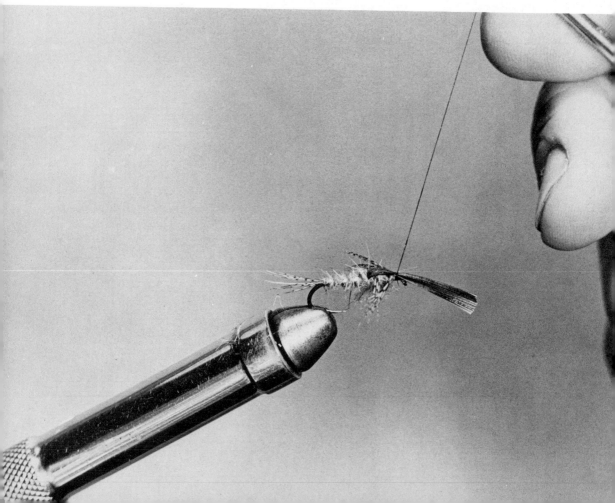

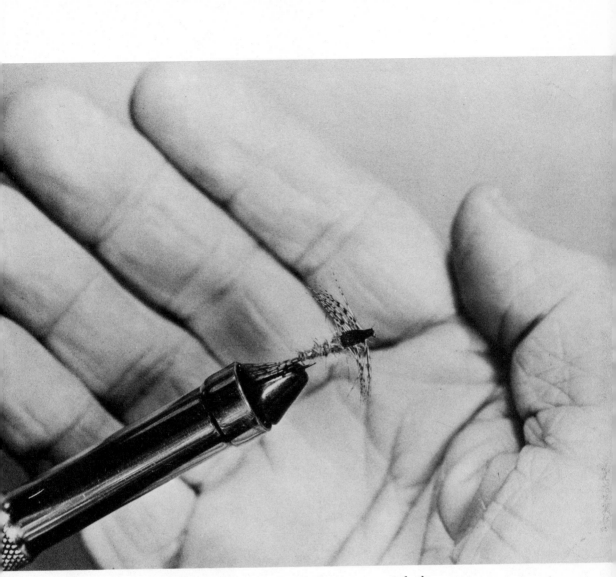

16 Complete the whip finish, apply head cement, and the nymph is done.

QUILL BODY EMERGER—WEIGHTED

Materials used

Hook: #10 to #14 2X Model Perfect wet fly
Tail: dark dun hackle fibers
Body: peacock quill, stripped, over
  lead wire
Thorax: peacock herl
Wing case: mallard shoulder feather, trimmed

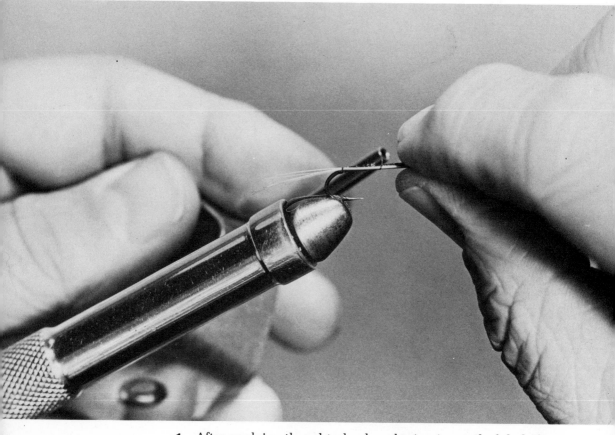

1   After applying thread to hook and tying in a tail of dark dun hackle fibers, cut a 3-inch piece of medium-width lead wire and place it alongside the hook shank on the near side, with one end at the bend of the hook. Make a few wraps to fasten in place.

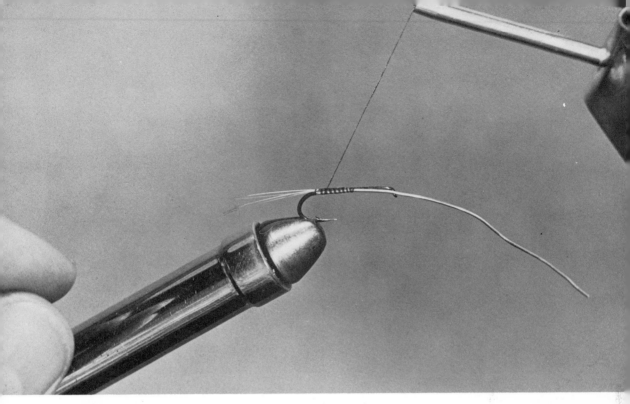

2   The wire can then be released with the fingers and more wraps made to position it securely on the shank.

3   At a point where the front of the body will be, fold the wire over to the other side of the hook shank and position it alongside the hook and tie it in place with thread.

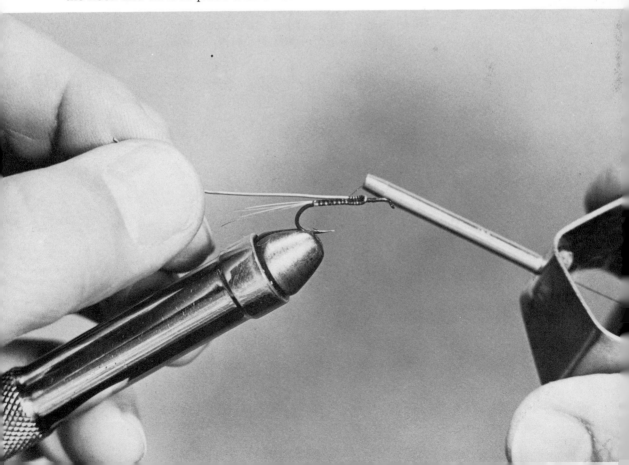

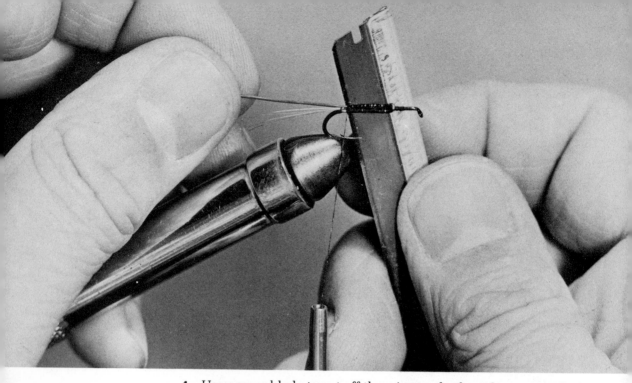

4 Use a razor blade to cut off the wire on the far side, even with the end of the wire on the near side. After cutting wire, wrap more thread over ends of wire to fill in the abrupt drop-off created by the ends of the wire.

5 This being a longer-bodied fly than most, more quill will be required to cover it completely. It will probably take two quills from a peacock eye, stripped with a pencil eraser as described in the instructions for tying the Quill Gordon dry fly. Tie in beneath hook at bend, with the dark stripe in position to show when wrapped.

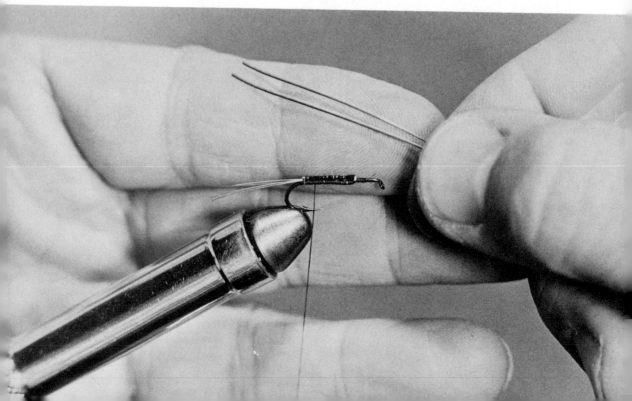

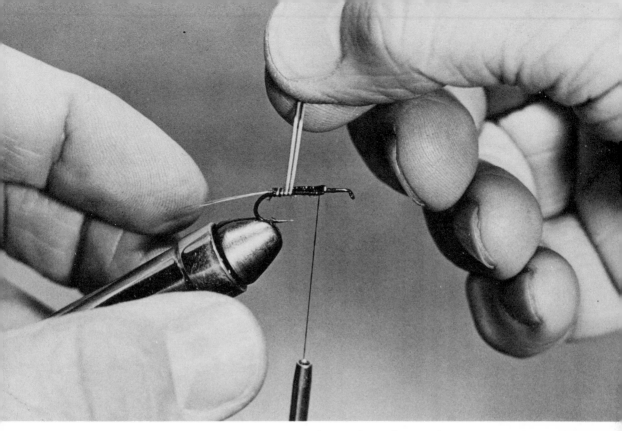

6 Grasp the two quills together, wrap forward to the point where the lead wire has crossed the hook shank, and tie off.

7 Tie off and remove stubs of quills.

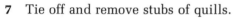

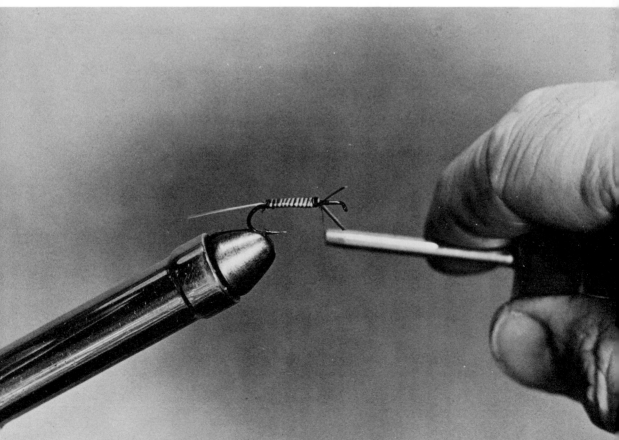

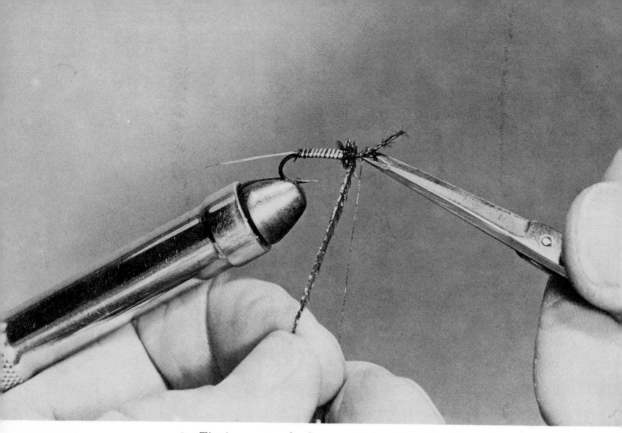

8 Tie in a strand of peacock herl by the tip and wrap on a thorax as shown.

9 Remove a bunch of about 12 hackle fibers from a large dark dun hackle feather and measure to determine the point where they can be tied in to reach the hook point.

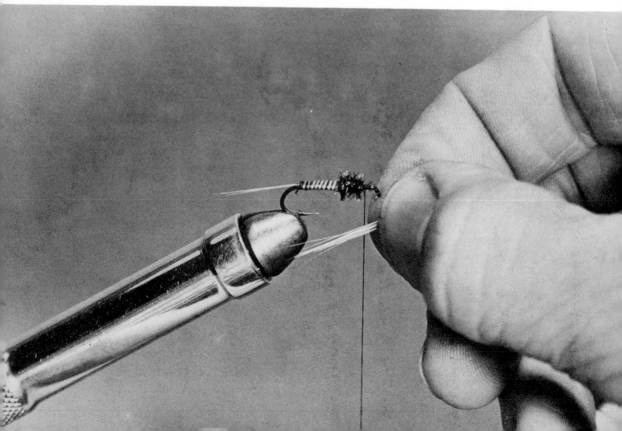

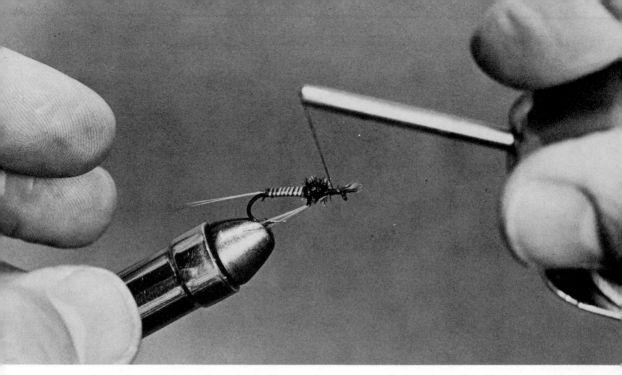

10   If you have diligently mastered procedures up to this point, your dexterity should enable you to apply the hackle-fiber beard without inverting the hook. The beard is tied in just as wings are tied in (Procedure 2), except that it goes beneath the shank rather than on top.

11   The wing case for this emerger type of nymph is made from a feather taken from the shoulder of a mallard wing. Tweezers or hackle pliers facilitate removal of a single feather from the wing.

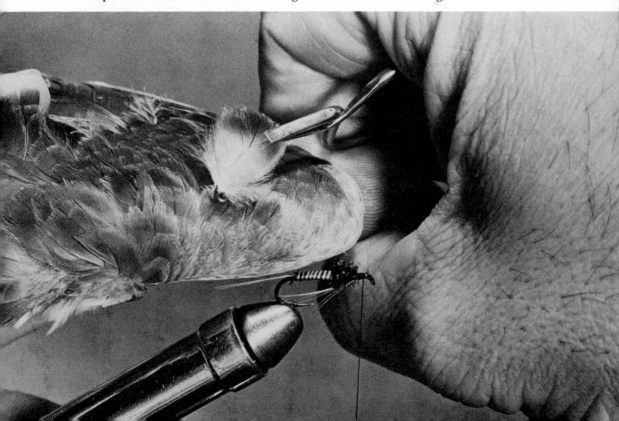

12 Cut the stem about halfway up, leaving a notch as shown. Next, cut the fibers off the lower stem, leaving stubs to help keep the feather from twisting during the tying-in step.

13 Hold the feather in place with the left hand, leaving space for the head, and make a few turns of thread lightly over the stem.

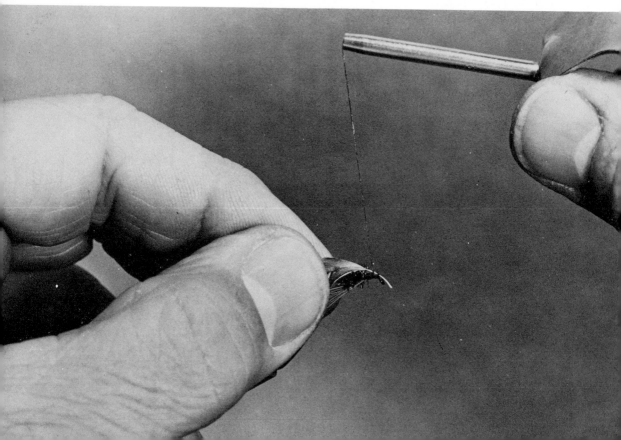

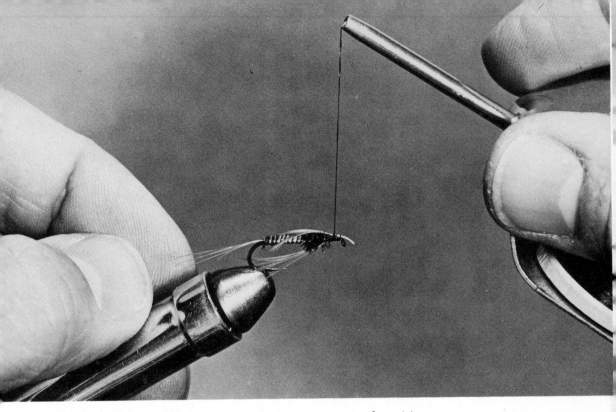

14 Release grip, and if feather does not rotate out of position, grasp it again with left hand and make three more wraps, but tightly, to secure it in position.

15 Snip off the stem, wrap the head, complete whip finish, and apply head cement.

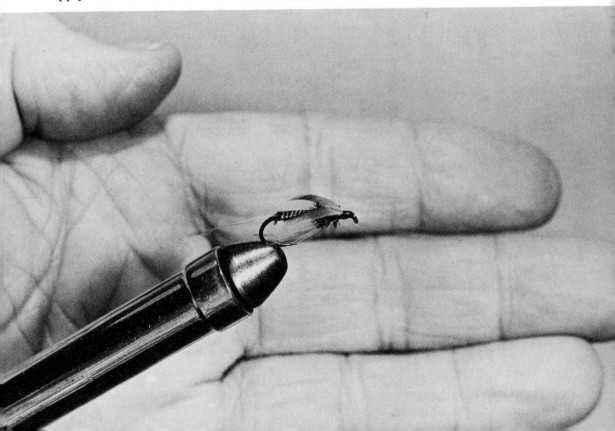

Appendix

SELECTED BIBLIOGRAPHY

THE TWO BOOKS IN MY OWN LIBRARY WHICH SHOW THE MOST wear are *Flies*, by J. Edson Leonard (New York: Barnes, 1950); and *The Fly and the Fish*, by John Atherton (New York: Macmillan, 1951). As a fly-fisherman and a fly-tier, I have found in them the happiest approach to the sport.

Next, *Matching the Hatch*, by Ernest Schwiebert (New York: Macmillan, 1955), shows great wear and tear and is invaluable for its entomological information and fly patterns.

Then, not in any particular order of preference, I find the following on my shelves: *The Complete Fly-Tyer*, by Reuben R. Cross (New York: Dodd, Mead, 1950); *Streamside Guide to Naturals and Their Imitations*, by Art Flick (New York: Putnam, 1947); *How to Fish from Top to Bottom*, by Sid Gordon (Harrisburg: Stackpole, 1955, out of print); *Fishing Flies and Fly Tying*, by William F. Blades (Harrisburg: Stackpole, 1951, out of print); *Streamer Fly Tying and Fishing*, by Col. Joe Bates (Harrisburg: Stackpole, 1966); *The Art of Tying the Wet Fly and Fishing the Flymph*, by James E. Leisenring and Vernon S. Hidy (New York: Crown, 1971); *A Book of Trout Flies*, by Preston J. Jennings (New York: Derrydale, 1935; Crown, 1970); *A Modern Dry-Fly Code*, by Vincent Marinaro (New York: Putnam, 1950; Crown, 1970); *Fishing the Nymph*, by Jim Quick (New York: Ronald, 1960); *Practical Fly-Fishing*, by Charles M. Wetzel (Boston: Christopher, 1943, out of print); *Nymphs*, by Ernest Schwiebert (New York: Winchester, 1972); *Dressing Flies for Fresh and Salt Water*, by Poul Jorgensen (Rockville Centre, N.Y.: Freshet); *Selective Trout*, by Doug Swisher and Carl Richards (New York: Crown, 1971); and *Fly Tying Materials*, by Eric Leiser (New York: Crown, 1972).

The Western fly-tier will enjoy *Tying and Fishing the Fuzzy*

Nymphs, by E. H. (Polly) Rosborough (Manchester, N.H.: Orvis, 1969); *Northwest Angling,* by Enos Bradner (Portland, Ore.: Binsfords & Mort); *Steelhead,* by Mel Marshall (New York: Winchester, 1973); and *Kamloops,* by Steve Raymond (New York: Winchester, 1972). *Western Trout Fly Tying Manual* by Jack Dennis (Jackson Hole, Wyo.: Snake River Books) is very handy. *Creative Fly-Tying and Fly-Fishing,* by Rex Gerlach (New York: Winchester, 1974), while not yet on the market at this writing, is highly recommended based on galleys and includes many Western as well as Eastern patterns.

British books which I have learned a great deal from include *An Angler's Entomology,* by J. R. Harris (South Brunswick: Barnes, 1952); *Nymphs and the Trout,* by Frank Sawyer (London: Stanley Paul, 1958); *Trout Fly Recognition,* by John Goddard (London: Black, 1966); and *The Way of a Trout with a Fly,* by G. E. M. Skues (London: Black, 1921).

For the saltwater fly-fisherman, there are *Saltwater Fly Fishing,* by Joe Brooks (New York: Putnam, 1950, out of print); and *Salt Water Flies,* by Kenneth E. Bay (Philadelphia: Lippincott, 1972).

SOME SOURCES OF FLY-TYING
MATERIALS AND EQUIPMENT

Dan Bailey
Box 1019
Livingston, Montana 59047

Mrs. Virginia Buszek
805 W. Tulare Ave.
Visalia, California 93277

Cortland Line Co. — Certified Pro Shops
(All over USA) Main Office: Cortland, New York

E. B. & H. A. Darbee
Livingston Manor, New York 12758

Fly Fisherman's Bookcase Tackle Service
Rte. 9A at Furnace Dock Rd.
Croton-on-Hudson, New York 10520

Bud Lilly Trout Shop
P. O. Box 387
West Yellowstone, Montana 59758

Orvis Company
Manchester, Vermont 02524

Reed Tackle
Box 390
Caldwell, New Jersey 07006